healthy indian
cooking

healthy indian
cooking

SHEHZAD HUSAIN AND MANISHA KANANI

southwater

This edition is published by Southwater, an imprint of Anness Publishing Ltd,
108 Great Russell Street, London WC1B 3NA; info@anness.com

www.southwaterbooks.com; www.annesspublishing.com

If you like the images in this book and would like to investigate using them for publishing, promotions or advertising,
please visit our website www.practicalpictures.com for more information.

© Anness Publishing Limited 2014

A CIP catalogue record for this book is available from the British Library.

Publisher: Joanna Lorenz
Editor: Ruth Baldwin
Designer: Sarah Kidd
Photography: David Jordon, David Armstrong and Ferguson Hill
Stylists: Judy Williams, Kay McGlone and Blake Minton
Nutritional Data: Wendy Doyle

NOTES
Bracketed terms are intended for American readers.
For all recipes, quantities are given in both metric and imperial measures and, where appropriate,
in standard cups and spoons. Follow one set of measures, but not a mixture, because they are not interchangeable.
Standard spoon and cup measures are level. 1 tsp = 5ml, 1 tbsp = 15ml, 1 cup = 250ml/8fl oz.
Australian standard tablespoons are 20ml. Australian readers should use 3 tsp in place of 1 tbsp for measuring small quantities.
American pints are 16fl oz/2 cups. American readers should use 20fl oz/2.5 cups in place of 1 pint when measuring liquids.
Electric oven temperatures in this book are for conventional ovens. When using a fan oven, the temperature will
probably need to be reduced by about 10–20°C/20–40°F. Since ovens vary, you should check with
your manufacturer's instruction book for guidance.
The nutritional analysis given for each recipe is calculated per portion (i.e. serving or item), unless otherwise stated.
If the recipe gives a range, such as Serves 4–6, then the nutritional analysis will be for the smaller portion size, i.e. 6 servings.
The analysis does not include optional ingredients, such as salt added to taste.
Medium (US large) eggs are used unless otherwise stated.

PUBLISHER'S NOTE

Contents

INTRODUCTION

There is now widespread agreement on healthy eating and the message is fairly straightforward: eat less fat, especially saturated fat, less sugar, less salt and more fibre. Loosely translated, this means eating more vegetables, fruit, complex carbohydrate foods such as rice, bread and pasta (preferably unrefined or wholegrain varieties), more fish, leaner meats and poultry without skin. With all these pleasurable foods to choose from, healthy eating should never be regarded as dull or uninteresting. Food should be a pleasure to cook and a joy to eat.

It is not difficult to see why Indian cooking can be healthy and low fat, as today the best of its cookery includes many of the recommended healthy foods. It uses lean, trimmed meat rather than fattier cuts, poultry with the skin removed, copious amounts of fresh vegetables and wholefoods, such as lentils and pulses, and nearly every meal is served with either rice or bread, and sometimes both. The one area in which Indian cookery has not met these requirements until recently is in its liberal use of pure ghee (clarified butter). But, as people become more aware of the importance of reducing fat in their diet, they are replacing vegetable oils for ghee in much of their Indian cooking, and cutting down on the quantities used.

The changes in diet promoted in this book are not designed to be dramatic. The amount of vegetable oil used for cooking has been greatly reduced, and low or reduced fat ingredients have been specified wherever possible. In particular, the more unhealthy, saturated fat, which comes principally from animal sources, such as dairy foods and fatty meats, has been avoided or drastically reduced. Where oil is used for cooking, corn oil is recommended, although any vegetable-based oil can be substituted. But remember always to fry over a fairly low heat if you are using less fat, as there is a higher chance of burning whatever you are frying, and use a non-stick frying pan wherever possible. Where lamb is used in recipes, it is recommended that you use spring lamb, as not only is this leaner and quicker to cook, but it also has a good flavour which helps achieve a more delicious end result.

Every gram of fat provides 9 kilocalories – more than twice the number from 1 gram of protein or carbohydrate. For those concerned about calorie intake, there is the added advantage that in lowering the fat content of traditional recipes the calorie content will also be reduced considerably. Experts recommend that no more than 30–33 per cent of our calories should come from fat. Based on a 2,000 kilocalorie-a-day diet, this means reducing the amount of fat from approximately 100 grams a day to 67–70 grams. We have chosen to take one-fifth of that amount (14 grams) as a cut-off point for one serving of the recipes in this book.

Natural low fat yogurt is used in many of the recipes as a healthier alternative to cream. It is a wonderful tenderizer and gives curries a thick, creamy texture. Always beat the yogurt with a fork first, then add it to the pan gradually over a low heat, stirring continuously to prevent it from curdling. Alternatively, stir 10ml/2 tsp of cornflour (cornstarch) into 15ml/1 tbsp of water, add to 600ml/1 pint/2½ cups of yogurt and stir well. Pour into a pan, bring to simmering point and simmer gently for 10 minutes before adding the yogurt to the recipe. If you use goats' milk yogurt, this will not curdle when added to hot food. But remember that the fat level of your dish will be higher, and use low fat versions wherever possible.

Fromage frais or crème fraîche in its virtually fat-free version is also used. Herbs and spices, which are an essential part of Indian and Pakistani cooking, are another very useful healthy addition as they contain no fat and also add plenty of flavour and colour to dishes.

Balti techniques, in particular, lend themselves well to low-fat cooking – and the recipes have the added advantage of being quick and easy to prepare. Balti is essentially a way of cooking a wide range of curries rapidly on top of the stove over a high heat using the stir-fry method and a wok-shaped cooking vessel with ring handles on either side, called a karahi. But to be able to reduce the amount of fat and still achieve the stunningly flavoursome Balti dishes that appear in this book, a non-stick wok is recommended.

The recipes have been made as simple and uncomplicated as possible, allowing you to enjoy these dishes any time of the week. They also show that the fat content of traditional recipes can be easily and effectively reduced without sacrificing the exotic flavours and aromas of Indian fare, so you can enjoy many delicious Indian meals without guilt.

Right: fresh vegetables, rice and shellfish are all used in this book to make healthy low fat Indian dishes.

INGREDIENTS

HERBS AND SPICES

The spices used in a dish are integral to its flavour and aroma. One spice can completely alter the taste of a dish and a combination of several will also affect its colour and texture. The quantities of spices and salt specified in this book are merely a guide, so feel free to experiment and increase and decrease these as you wish. This is particularly true of fresh chillies and chilli powder: experiment with quantities, adding less than specified if wished.

Bay leaves The large dried leaves of the bay laurel tree are among the oldest herbs used in cooking and go well in meat and rice dishes (1).
Cardamom pods This spice is native to India, where it is the most prized spice after saffron. The pale green and beige pods have a finer flavour than the coarser brown ones. The pods can be used whole or the husks can be removed to release the seeds. They have a slightly pungent, very aromatic taste (2).
Chillies – dried These peppers are extremely fiery and should be used with caution. You can remove the seeds from dried chillies to lessen their heat. Dried chillies can be used whole or coarsely crushed (3).
Chilli powder Also known as cayenne pepper, this fiery ground spice should be used with caution. the heat varies from brand to brand, so adjust quantities to your taste (4).
Cinnamon One of the earliest known spices, cinnamon has an aromatic and sweet flavour. It is sold ground and as sticks. The sticks are used for flavour and are not eaten (5).

Right: shown clockwise from top left are coriander (cilantro), mint, bay leaves, fenugreek and curry leaves.

Cloves This spice is used to flavour many sweet and savoury dishes and is usually added whole. It is also used in spice mixtures like garam masala (6).
Coriander (Cilantro) – leaves, seeds and powder This aromatic spice has a pungent, slightly sweet lemony flavour. The seeds are used widely, either coarsely ground or in powdered form, in meat, fish and poultry dishes. Ground coriander, a brownish powder, is an important constituent of any mixture of curry spices. Fresh coriander is a beautifully fragrant herb, used in cooking and sprinkled over dishes as a garnish (7).
Cumin "White" cumin seeds are oval, ridged, and greenish brown in colour. They have a strong aroma and flavour and can be used whole or ground. Ready-ground cumin is widely available. Black cumin seeds, less easy to find, are dark and aromatic and are used to flavour curries and rice and seasonings (8).
Curry leaves Similar in appearance to bay leaves but with a very different flavour, these can be bought dried, and occasionally fresh, from Asian stores. Fresh leaves freeze well (9).

Curry powder There are many variations of this popular and convenient spice mixture, varying both in flavour and colour (10).
Fennel seeds Very similar in appearance to cumin seeds, fennel seeds have a sweet, aniseed taste and are used to flavour some curries. They can be chewed as a mouth-freshener after a spicy meal (11).
Fenugreek – seeds and fresh These flat, extremely pungent and slightly bitter seeds are used in spice mixtures. The fresh leaves are used to flavour meat and vegetarian dishes. Always discard the stalks which will make the dish bitter (12).
Garam masala This is a mixture of spices which can be made from freshly ground spices at home or purchased ready-made. There is no set recipe, but a typical mixture might include black cumin seeds, peppercorns, cloves, cinnamon and black cardamom pods (13).
Garlic This is a standard ingredient, along with ginger, in most curries. It can be used crushed or chopped. The powder is mainly used in spice mixtures (14).

Ginger One of the most popular spices in India, and also one of the oldest, fresh ginger is an important ingredient in many curries and is now widely available. It should always be peeled before use. Dried ginger is a useful standby (15).

Mustard seeds Round in shape, sharp-tasting mustard seeds are used to flavour a variety of curries and relishes (16).

Nutmeg Whole and ground, nutmeg has a sweet, nutty flavour (17).

Onion seeds Black in colour and triangular in shape, these seeds are widely used in pickles and to flavour vegetable curries.

Paprika A rust-red powder which has a sweetish pungent taste and adds a good colour (18).

Peppercorns Black peppercorns are sometimes used whole with other whole spices, such as cloves, cardamom pods and bay leaves, to flavour curries. Otherwise, whenever possible, use freshly ground or crushed black pepper (19).

Poppy seeds These whole seeds are usually toasted to bring out the full flavour of curries.

Saffron The world's most expensive spice is the dried stigmas of the saffron crocus, which is native to Asia Minor. Needed only in small quantities to flavour and colour a dish, it has a beautiful flavour and aroma. It is sold both as strands and in a powder form (20).

Sesame seeds These are small, cream-coloured seeds with a slightly nutty taste (21).

Tamarind The tamarind pod is dried to form a dark brown, sticky pulp which is soaked in hot water, then strained before use. It has a strong, sour taste and is used in curries and chutneys (22).

Turmeric This bright yellow, bitter-tasting spice is sold ground. It is used mainly for colour rather than to add flavour to a dish (23).

PULSES, LENTILS AND RICE

Pulses and lentils play an important role in Indian cooking and are a good source of protein. Some are cooked whole, some are puréed and made into soups or "dhals" and some are combined with vegetables or meat. Rice is served with almost every Indian meal so Indians have created a variety of ways of cooking it, each quite distinctive. Basmati rice is the most popular type. Plain boiled rice is an everyday accompaniment; for entertaining, it is combined with other ingredients to make a more interesting dish.

Black-eyed beans Sometimes called black-eyed peas, these small cream-coloured beans have a black spot or "eye". When cooked, they have a tender creamy texture and a mildly smoky flavour. They are used widely in Indian cooking.

Chickpeas These round, beige-coloured pulses have a strong, nutty flavour when cooked. As well as being used for curries, they are also ground into a flour which is widely used in many Indian dishes such as pakoras and bhajees and are also added to Indian snacks.

Chana dhal This is a round, yellow split lentil, similar in appearance to the smaller *moong dhal* and the larger yellow split pea, which can be used as a substitute. It is used in a variety of vegetable dishes and can also be deep-fried and mixed with Indian crisps and spices, as in Bombay mix. It is used as a binding agent in some dishes.

Below: pictured clockwise from top left are black-eyed beans (peas), haricot beans, chickpeas, flageolet beans, mung beans and red kidney beans.

COOKING PLAIN BOILED RICE

Wash all varieties of rice in several changes of water and leave to soak before cooking.

To cook plain boiled rice, always make sure you use a tight-fitting lid for your rice pan. If you do not have one that fits tightly enough, either wrap a dish towel round the lid or put some foil between the lid and the pan. Try not to remove the lid until the rice is cooked. (The advantage of using just a lid is that you can tell when the rice is ready because steam begins to escape, visibly and rapidly.)

For four people, you will need 450g/ 1lb/1½ cups basmati rice. Wash it thoroughly until the water runs clear. Place in a heavy pan and add 5ml/1tsp salt and 750ml/1¼ pints/3 cups of water. Bring to the boil, turn the heat very low and cover. Cook for 10–12 minutes.

Before serving, move the rice grains about gently with a slotted spoon to introduce air – a slotted spoon will prevent you from breaking up the grains, which would make the rice mushy and unattractive.

As a rough serving guide for portions, allow about 75g/3oz/scant ½ cup of rice per person.

Flageolet beans These are small oval beans which are either white or pale green in colour. They have a very mild, refreshing flavour.

Green lentils Also known as continental lentils, these lentils have quite a strong flavour and retain their shape and colour during cooking. They are very versatile and are used in a number of dishes.

Haricot (navy) beans Small, white oval beans which come in different varieties, haricot beans are ideal for Indian cooking because not only do they retain their shape, but they also absorb the flavours of the spices.

Kidney beans Kidney beans are one of the most popular pulses used in Indian cooking. They are dark red-brown, kidney-shaped beans with a strong flavour.

***Masoor dhal* (red split lentils)** These split red lentils are actually orange in colour and turn a pale yellow when cooked. Whole brown lentils are a type of red lentil with the husk intact. They can be used for

Above: Basmati rice is the most popular type of rice eaten with Indian food.

making dhal and as a replacement for *toovar dhal*.

Moong dhal This teardrop-shaped split yellow lentil is similar to, though smaller than, *chana dhal*.

Mung beans These are very small, round, green beans with a slightly sweet flavour and creamy texture. When sprouted, they produce the familiar bean sprouts. Split mung beans are also used in Indian cooking and are often cooked with rice to make a popular Gujarati dish.

Rice This is an annual cereal grass with many varieties. Different types of rice produce a different texture when cooked. Basmati rice, a long-grained milled white rice grown in both India and Pakistan, is the most popular type eaten with Indian food as it has a distinctive aromatic flavour, cooks very well and gives an excellent finished result.

Toor dhal This is a shiny, yellow, split lentil, similar in size to *chana dhal*.

Toovar dhal A dull orange-coloured split pea with a very distinctive earthy flavour. *Toovar dhal* is available plain and in an oily variety.

Urid dhal Also known as black gram, this lentil is similar in size to *moong dhal* and is available either with the blackish hull retained or with it removed.

VEGETABLES

Indian cooking specializes in many different ways of using vegetables, which include everything from cauliflower, potatoes and peas to more exotic and unusual varieties, such as okra and bitter gourds. When it comes to Indian cooking, fresh vegetables are indispensable.

Aubergines (eggplants) Available in different varieties, the shiny deep purple aubergine is the most common and widely used variety in Indian cooking. Aubergines have a strong flavour with a slightly bitter taste and are sometimes sprinkled with salt to extract some of these bitter juices.

Bitter gourds One of the many very bitter vegetables often used in Indian cooking, this long, knobbly green vegetable comes from Kenya and has a strong, distinct taste. To prepare a gourd, peel the ridged skin with a sharp knife, scrape away and discard the seeds and chop the flesh.

Cauliflower A large round vegetable with creamy white flowers and green leaves, this versatile vegetable is very popular in Indian cooking because it absorbs the flavour of spices well. It is often combined with other vegetables, particularly with potatoes.

Chillies – fresh Much of the severe heat of fresh chillies is contained in the seeds, and can be lessened by splitting the chillies and washing away the seeds in cold running water. Wash your hands thoroughly with soap and water after handling cut chillies and avoid touching your face – particularly your lips and eyes – for a good while afterwards.

Corn Corn originated in America but is now grown all over the world. Corn on the cob has a delicious sweet, juicy flavour which is at its best just after picking. Canned corn, is a more convenient alternative.

Okra Also known as ladies' fingers, okra is one of the most popular Indian vegetables. These small green five-sided pods have a very distinctive flavour and a sticky, pulpy texture when cooked.

Onions A popular root vegetable belonging to the allium family, onions have a strong pungent flavour and aroma. Globe onions are the most commonly used variety for Indian cooking. Spring onions (scallions) are also used in some dishes for their mild taste. Red onions, deep purple in colour, are more pungent than the white varieties.

Red (Bell) Peppers These are large hollow pods belonging to the capsicum family and are also available in other colours, including green, yellow, orange, white and even black. Red peppers are slightly sweeter than green peppers. They are used in a variety of Indian dishes, adding colour and flavour.

Spinach Available all the year round, this green leafy vegetable has a mild delicate flavour. The leaves do vary in size but only the large thick leaves need to be trimmed of their stalks. Spinach is a popular vegetable in Indian cooking – in India there are over 15 different varieties. It is cooked in many ways, both with meat and other vegetables.

Tomatoes Tomatoes are available all year round in a variety of colours ranging from red to orange, yellow to green. They are widely used to add colour, flavour nd texture to numerous dishes. They are an essential ingredient in Indian cooking and are used to make all sorts of sauces, chutneys and relishes.

Right: vegetables are an essential ingredient in many Indian dishes.

COOKING EQUIPMENT AND UTENSILS

Balloon whisk A metal whisk useful for beating yoghurt before cooking.

Chappati griddle (*tava*) A heavy wrought iron frying pan that allows chappatis and other breads to be cooked without burning. Can also be used for cooking spices (1).

Chappati rolling board (*roti takata*) This board consists of a round wooden surface on stubby legs and helps in shaping different sizes of breads. The extra height helps disperse excess dry flour (2).

Chappati rolling pin (*velan*) This is thinner in shape than Western pins and come in many sizes. Use whichever best suits your hand (3).

Chappati spoon (*roti chamcha*) The square-shaped flat head assists in roasting breads on the hot griddle (4).

Coffee grinder Useful for grinding small quantities of ingredients, particularly spices.

Colander (*channi*) Use a sturdy, stainless steel colander as it will not discolour like plastic (5).

Food processor This is an essential piece of equipment. Smaller amounts of ingredients can be ground with a pestle and mortar (6).

Heat diffuser Many curries are simmered gently over a low heat, and a heat diffuser helps prevent burning on the base (7).

Indian frying pan (*karahi*) A karahi is similar to a wok but is more rounded in shape and is made of heavier metal. It is the traditional cooking vessel for Balti dishes, although for low-fat recipes a non-stick wok is recommended as an alternative (8).

Knives (*churrie*) Keep knives sharp. It will be easier to chop ingredients and will ensure neat edges (9).

Non-stick frying pan A frying pan with a non-stick coating makes it possible to fry ingredients using much

less fat than usual and is recommended for the recipes in this book.

Oblong grinding stone and pin (*sil padi*) This is a traditional Indian "food processor". The ingredients are placed on a stone made of heavy slate marked with notches. The rolling pin is used to pulverize the ingredients against the stone (10).

Pastry brush This provides a good way of brushing meat and vegetables lightly with oil before grilling.

Rice spoon (*chawal ke chamchi*) This prevents the rice grains from being damaged while serving (11).

Sizzler (*garam thali*) This enables food to be served at the table while it is still cooking (12).

Slotted spoon (*channi chamchi*) This enables items to be removed safely from deep hot oil or other liquids; also used for stirring rice (13).

Stainless steel mortar and pestle (*hamam dasta*) This is ideal for

grinding small amounts of wet ingredients such as ginger and garlic. The steel is everlasting and will not retain the strong flavours of the spices (14).

Stone pestle mortar and pestle (*pathar hamam dasta*) This is suitable for mixing small amounts of ingredients, both wet and dry (15).

Wok This is a good substitute for a karahi if reducing the amount of cooking oil in frying, particularly when coated with a non-stick layer.

BASIC RECIPES

Coconut Milk

Coconut milk is used to enrich and flavour many dishes in the Far East and is needed for several recipes in this book. It should be used sparingly as it has a very high fat content. When choosing a coconut, shake the nut firmly. If you cannot hear the milk sloshing around, the flesh will be difficult to remove. A coconut with its green husk and fibre attached will almost certainly have soft and creamy white flesh. Fresh coconut milk will keep refrigerated for up to two days.

INGREDIENTS

Makes 1.2 litres/2 pints/5 cups
2 fresh coconuts
1.2 litres/2 pints/5 cups of water, off the boil

1 Hold the coconut over a bowl to collect the liquid. With the back of a large knife or cleaver, crack open the coconut by striking it cleanly.

2 Scrape out the white meat with a citrus zester or a rounded butter curler. Place the coconut meat in a food processor with half of the water.

3 Process for 1 minute, then pass through a food mill or *mouli* fitted with a fine disk, catching the milk in a bowl beneath. Alternatively, squeeze the coconut meat with your hands and press through a nylon sieve (strainer). Place the coconut meat in a food processor with the rest of the water, blend and press for a second time. Allow the milk to settle for 30 minutes (creamy solids will rise to the surface). Sometimes the solids should be poured off and added later as a thickener.

BREADS

Most traditional Indian breads are unleavened; that is, they do not contain any raising agent and are made with a special ground wholemeal flour, known as *atta*.

Chappati

This is the staple bread of northern and central India. Chappatis are very thin, flat, unleavened bread made from ground wholemeal flour, traditionally cooked on a hot *tava*. They have a light texture and are fairly bland.

INGREDIENTS

Makes 10–12
350g/12oz/3 cups *atta* wholemeal (whole-wheat) flour
5ml/1 tsp salt
water, to mix
a little vegetable oil, for brushing

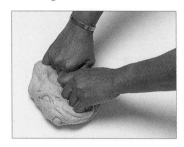

1 Sift the flour and salt into a large bowl. Make a well in the centre and slowly add small quantities of water until you have a smooth but pliable dough. Grease the palms of your hands and knead the dough well. Keep covered until you are ready to use.

2 Divide the dough into 10–12 equal portions, using one portion at a time and keeping the rest covered. Knead each portion into a ball, then flatten with your hands and place on a floured surface. Roll out the dough until you have a circle about 18cm/7in in diameter.

3 Heat a heavy griddle and, when hot, cook the chappatis on each side, pressing the edges down gently. When both sides are cooked, brush the first side lightly with vegetable oil.

Left: Chappatis (top) and naan (bottom) are two of the less fattening Indian breads.

1 Pre-heat the oven to 200°C/ 400°F/Gas 6. Mix the yeast, warm milk and sugar and leave to become frothy. Sift the flour, baking powder and salt. Make a well and fold in the yeast, milk, yogurt, egg and oil.

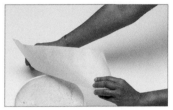

2 Knead the dough well. Tightly cover the bowl and keep in a warm place until the dough doubles in size. To test, push a finger into the dough – it should spring back. Roll out the dough on a floured surface.

3 Make each naan slipper-shaped, about 25cm/10in long and about 15cm/6in wide tapering to 5cm/2in. Sprinkle with the coriander leaves. Place on lightly greased trays and bake for 10–15 minutes.

Naan

Traditionally, naans are baked in a tandoor or clay oven, though grilled (broiled) naans look just as authentic. Naan is probably the most popular of all Indian breads. It is normally made with plain (all-purpose) flour enriched with yogurt and yeast, and can be eaten with most meat or vegetable dishes. Always serve naan warm, straight from the oven, or wrap in foil until you are ready to serve the meal. To keep the fat content of each naan down, you could make the naans smaller, using the recipe to make about 12 round naans.

INGREDIENTS

Makes 6–8
10ml/2 tsp yeast, active dried
60ml/4 tbsp warm milk
10ml/2 tsp sugar
450g/1lb/4 cups plain (all-purpose) flour
5ml/1 tsp baking powder
2.5ml/½ tsp salt
150ml/¼ pint/⅔ cup milk
150ml/¼ pint/⅔ cup low-fat natural
   (plain) yogurt, beaten
1 egg, beaten
15ml/1 tbsp vegetable oil
oil, for greasing
chopped coriander (cilantro) leaves

Basic Spice Mixtures

Most traditional Indian households use individual spices which are freshly ground and mixed, as needed.

Curry Powder

This is a mild curry powder, but you can adjust the spices to suit your taste.

Ingredients

Makes about 115g/4oz
Whole spices
50g/2oz/½ cup coriander seeds
60ml/4 tbsp cumin seeds
30ml/2 tbsp fennel seeds
30ml/2 tbsp fenugreek seeds
4 dried red chillies
5 curry leaves

Ground spices
15ml/1 tbsp chilli powder
15ml/1 tbsp turmeric
2.5ml/½ tsp salt

1 Dry-roast the whole spices in a large heavy pan for 8–10 minutes, shaking the pan from side to side until the slices begin to darken and release a rich aroma. Allow them to cool slightly.

***

_____ Cook's Tip _____

If you would like a hot curry powder then increase the quantity of dried red chillies.

2 Put the spices in a coffee grinder and grind to a fine powder.

3 Add the remaining ground spices and store in an airtight jar.

Garam Masala

Garam means "hot" and masala means "spices" and this mixture uses spices which "heat" the body, such as black peppercorns and cloves. Garam masala is added at the end of cooking and is also sprinkled over dishes as a garnish.

Ingredients

Makes about 50g/2oz
10 dried red chillies
3 x 2.5cm/1in cinnamon sticks
2 curry leaves
30ml/2 tbsp coriander seeds
30ml/2 tbsp cumin seeds
5ml/1 tsp black peppercorns
5ml/1 tsp cloves
5ml/1 tsp fenugreek seeds
5ml/1 tsp black mustard seeds
1.5ml/¼ tsp chilli powder

1 Dry-roast the chillies, cinnamon sticks and curry leaves in a large heavy frying pan or wok for 2 minutes.

2 Add the coriander and cumin seeds, peppercorns, cloves, fenugreek and mustard seeds and dry-roast the spices for 8–10 minutes, shaking the pan from side to side until the spices begin to darken in colour and release a rich aroma.

3 Allow the mixture to cool slightly, then put the spices into a coffee grinder or use a mortar and pestle and grind to a fine powder. Add the chilli powder, mix and store in an airtight jar.

_____ Cook's Tip _____

The Curry Powder and Garam Masala will keep for 2–4 months in an airtight container where their flavours will mature.

Curry Paste

A curry paste is a "wet" blend of spices cooked with oil and vinegar which help to preserve the spices. It is a quick and convenient way of adding a mixture of spices, and as you only need to add a small amount it will add minimal fat to a recipe.

INGREDIENTS

Makes about 600ml/1 pint/2½ cups
50g/2oz/½ cup coriander seeds
60ml/4 tbsp cumin seeds
30ml/2 tbsp fennel seeds
30ml/2 tbsp fenugreek seeds
4 dried red chillies
5 curry leaves
15ml/1 tbsp chilli powder
15ml/1 tbsp turmeric
150ml/¼ pint/⅔ cup wine vinegar
250ml/8fl oz/1 cup oil

1 Grind the whole spices to a fine powder. Spoon into a bowl and add the remaining ground spices.

2 Mix all the ground spices with the vinegar and add 75ml/5 tbsp water to form a thin paste.

3 Heat the oil in a large heavy frying pan and stir-fry the spice paste for 10 minutes or until all the water has been absorbed. When the oil rises to the surface the paste is cooked. Allow to cool slightly before spooning into sterilized jars.

_____ COOK'S TIP _____

Once the paste has been cooked, heat a little more oil and pour on top of the paste into the jar. This will help to preserve the paste and stop any mould from forming as the oil will stay on top as the paste is used.

Tikka Paste

A delicious, versatile paste which can be used in a variety of dishes.

INGREDIENTS

Makes about 475ml/16fl oz/2 cups
30ml/2 tbsp coriander seeds
30ml/2 tbsp cumin seeds
25ml/1½ tbsp garlic powder
30ml/2 tbsp paprika
15ml/1 tbsp garam masala
15ml/1 tbsp ground ginger
10ml/2 tsp chilli powder
2.5ml/½ tsp turmeric
15ml/1 tbsp dried mint
1.5ml/¼ tsp salt
5ml/1 tsp lemon juice
a few drops of red food colouring
a few drops of yellow food colouring
150 ml/¼ pint/⅔ cup wine vinegar
150ml/¼ pint/⅔ cup oil

1 Grind the coriander and cumin seeds to a fine powder using a coffee grinder or pestle and mortar. Spoon the mixture into a bowl and add the remaining spices, the mint and salt, stirring well.

2 Mix the spice powder with the lemon juice, food colourings and vinegar and add 30ml/2 tbsp water to form a thin paste.

3 Heat the oil in a large heavy frying pan and stir-fry the paste for 10 minutes or until all the water has been absorbed. When the oil rises to the surface, the paste is cooked. Allow the paste to cool slightly before spooning into sterilized jars.

Relishes and Chutneys

Dips and relishes are the perfect accompaniment to hot curries and spicy dishes. Some standard recipes are featured here, but others are included in the recipe section of the book.

Cucumber Raita

A cool, refreshing relish, ideal with curries or served as a dip with dishes such as kebabs.

Ingredients

Makes about 600ml/1 pint/2¹/₂ cups
½ cucumber
1 green chilli, seeded and finely
   chopped
300ml/½ pint/1¼ cups natural (plain)
   low fat yogurt
1.5ml/¼ tsp salt
1.5ml/¼ tsp ground cumin

1 Dice the cucumber finely and place in a bowl. Add the chilli.

2 Beat the yogurt with a fork until smooth and stir into the cucumber and chilli mixture.

3 Stir in the salt and cumin. Cover and chill before serving.

VARIATION

Instead of cucumber, use two skinned, seeded and chopped tomatoes and 15ml/ 1 tbsp chopped fresh coriander (cilantro).

Tomato and Chilli Chutney

If you like hot food this spicy tomato chutney is the perfect accompaniment.

Ingredients

Makes about 475ml/16fl oz/2 cups
4 tomatoes
1 red (bell) pepper
2 green chillies, roughly chopped
1 garlic clove, roughly chopped
1.5ml/¼ tsp salt
2.5ml/½ tsp sugar
5ml/1 tsp chilli powder
45ml/3 tbsp tomato purée (paste)
15ml/1 tbsp fresh coriander (cilantro),
   chopped

1 Roughly chop the tomatoes, which need not be de-seeded.

2 Halve the red pepper and remove the core and seeds. Roughly chop the red pepper halves.

3 Put all the ingredients into a food processor with 30ml/2 tbsp water and process until fairly smooth. Cover and chill until needed.

Coriander Chutney

A popular Indian side dish, this delicious chutney is made using fresh coriander (cilantro).

INGREDIENTS

Makes about 475ml/16fl oz/2 cups
115g/4oz fresh coriander (cilantro)
   leaves
1 green chilli
2 garlic cloves, roughly chopped
5ml/1 tsp salt
2.5ml/½ tsp sugar
25ml/1½ tbsp lemon juice

2 De-seed the chilli and roughly chop into small pieces.

1 Roughly chop the coriander leaves using a sharp knife.

3 Put all the ingredients into a food processor or blender together with 120ml/4fl oz/½ cup water and process until smooth. Cover and chill.

Mint and Coconut Chutney

INGREDIENTS

Makes about 350ml/12fl oz/1½ cups
50g/2oz fresh mint leaves
90ml/6 tbsp desiccated (dry unsweetened shredded) coconut
15ml/1 tbsp sesame seeds
1.5ml/¼ tsp salt
175ml/6fl oz/¾ cup natural (plain) low fat yogurt

1 Finely chop the mint using a sharp knife.

—— COOK'S TIP ——

This delicious chutney can be made in advance and will keep covered for up to 5 days in the refrigerator.

2 Put all the ingredients into a food processor or blender and process until smooth. Cover and chill.

BASIC TECHNIQUES

Crushed Fresh Root Ginger

Crushed ginger is specified in many of the dishes and it can be time-consuming to peel and process fresh root ginger for each individual recipe. It's much easier to make the crushed ginger in a large quantity and use it as needed.

1 Peel off the tough skin using a small sharp knife or potato peeler.

2 Roughly chop the ginger into fairly small pieces.

3 Process the pieces in a food processor or blender, adding a little water if necessary to get the right consistency. Store in an airtight container in the refrigerator for 4–6 weeks or freeze in ice-cube trays kept for the purpose (they will absorb some of the smell from the ginger).

Crushed Garlic

As with crushed ginger, it makes sense to prepare crushed garlic in reasonable quantities and store in the refrigerator or freezer until needed.

1 Separate the garlic into cloves and peel off the skin.

2 Process the whole cloves in a food processor or blender.

3 Freeze in ice-cube trays kept specially for the purpose. Put 5ml/1 tsp in each compartment, freeze, remove from the tray and store in the freezer in a plastic bag. Alternatively, store in an airtight container in the refrigerator for 4–6 weeks.

Freezing Fresh Coriander (Cilantro)

There is no substitute for fresh coriander (cilantro) and the more that is used in Indian cooking the better, as it imparts a beautiful flavour and aroma, particularly to Balti dishes. It is now readily available from most supermarkets and, more economically, from specialist Indian stores. If wished, you can buy a large quantity and freeze whatever you do not require immediately for future use.

1 Cut off the roots and any thick stalks, but leave the fine stalks.

2 Wash the leaves in cold water and leave in a strainer to drain.

3 When dry, chop the leaves and store them in plastic bags or airtight containers in the freezer. Do not defrost before using.

Chopping Herbs

Chop fresh herbs just before you need to add them to a dish.

1 Remove any thick stalks, then use a sharp knife to chop the leaves finely or snip with scissors in a cup.

2 Alternatively, use a herb chopper, also called a *mezzaluna*.

Seeding and Chopping Chillies

Wash your hands after preparing chillies, to remove the stinging juice. Where the recipes in this book specify two chillies, this will make the dish quite hot and you can reduce this number to taste. The small, fat chillies are milder than the long thin ones.

1 Cut the chillies in half lengthways, remove the membranes and seeds.

2 Cut the flesh lengthways into strips. Cut these into small dice.

Chopping Onions

Many of the Balti and curry dishes in this book use chopped onions as an essential flavouring, and for stir-fried dishes in particular it is important to keep the pieces even. This is a quick and easy way of cutting onions.

***

COOK'S TIP

To stop your eyes stinging whilst peeling onions, try peeling them under water.

***

1 Cut the onion in half, leaving the root intact, and carefully peel off the outer skin.

2 Place the cut side of the onion down and make horizontal cuts at 5mm/¼in intervals, making sure not to cut through the root.

3 Make vertical cuts in the same way at 5mm/¼in intervals.

4 Hold the onion firmly with one hand and carefully chop finely into small, even dice.

Browning Onions

The final colour and texture of a curry depends on how well you brown the onions during the first stage of cooking. This requires patience, especially as you will be cooking them in small quantities of oil.

1 Heat 15ml/1 tbsp of oil in a heavy pan or wok.

2 Add the chopped or sliced onions, then reduce the heat slightly. Stir the onions only occasionally; excessive stirring will draw the moisture from them and inhibit the browning process.

3 Continue cooking until the onions are evenly golden brown.

Preparing Poultry and Meat

Poultry and meat for low fat dishes need to be trimmed of all skin and visible fat, so that only the lean part is used in the recipe.

1 Always remove all the skin from chicken portions.

2 Buy lean cuts of lamb, then trim off any visible fat.

3 Cut into even-sized pieces for stir-frying. Cut the lamb into strips and the boned chicken into cubes.

Stir-frying

A non-stick wok or frying pan is best for cooking low-fat Indian dishes as it means that the quantity of oil used can be considerably reduced.

1 Always heat the wok or frying pan for a minute or so before adding the oil or any other ingredients. When adding the oil, swirl it into the wok and allow it to heat before adding the next ingredients.

2 When adding the first ingredients, reduce the heat a little. This will ensure that they are not overcooked or burnt by the time the remaining ingredients have been added.

3 Once all the ingredients have been added to the wok, quickly increase the heat to allow the dish to cook in the least possible time. This allows the ingredients to retain a crisp, fresh texture and prevents them from absorbing too much oil.

4 Use a large wooden spoon or a non-stick slotted spoon to turn the ingredients as you stir-fry.

5 To clean the wok, wipe out the inside with kitchen paper where possible, and keep washing with detergent to the barest minimum.

SOUPS
AND
APPETIZERS

If you like to serve an Indian meal in several courses,
Spiced Cauliflower Soup, Vegetable Samosas and Glazed
Garlic Shrimp make an ideal start to the menu –
mouthwatering and light, they will awaken the appetite without
being too filling. The dishes in this section are also ideal for
low fat lunches or suppertime snacks, although a number of the
other recipes in this book, particularly some of the vegetable
dishes, would be just as suitable for a light lunch or appetizer.

Tomato and Coriander Soup

Although soups are not often eaten in India or Pakistan, tomato soup seems to be among the most popular ones. It is excellent on a cold winter's day.

INGREDIENTS

Serves 4

675g/1½lb tomatoes, peeled
  and chopped
15ml/1 tbsp oil
1 bay leaf
4 spring onions (scallions), chopped
5ml/1 tsp salt
2.5ml/½ tsp crushed garlic
5ml/1 tsp crushed black peppercorns
30ml/2 tbsp chopped fresh coriander
  (cilantro)
750ml/1¼ pints/generous 3 cups water
15ml/1 tbsp cornflour (cornstarch)
30ml/2 tbsp single (light) cream, to
  garnish (optional)

NUTRITIONAL NOTES	
Per Portion	
Energy	76Kcals/315KJ
Fat	3.40g
Saturated Fat	0.43g
Carbohydrate	10.10g
Fibre	1.90g

――――― COOK'S TIP ―――――

If the only fresh tomatoes available are rather pale and under-ripe, add 15ml/ 1 tbsp tomato purée (paste) to the pan with the chopped tomatoes to enhance the colour and flavour of the soup.

1 To skin the tomatoes, plunge them in very hot water, then take them out more or less straight away. The skin should now peel off easily. If not, put the tomatoes back in the water for a little longer. Once this is done, roughly chop the tomatoes.

2 In a medium pan, heat the oil and fry the tomatoes, bay leaf and spring onions for a few minutes until soft.

3 Gradually add the salt, garlic, peppercorns and coriander and water. Simmer gently over a low heat for 15–20 minutes.

4 Meanwhile, dissolve the cornflour in a little cold water to form a thick creamy paste.

5 Remove the soup from the heat and allow to cool slightly for a few minutes. Strain the soup, or liquidize using a food processor.

6 Return the puréed soup to the pan, add the cornflour mixture and stir over a gentle heat for about 3 minutes until thickened.

7 Pour the soup into individual serving dishes and garnish with a swirl of cream, if using. Serve hot.

Spiced Cauliflower Soup

Light and tasty, this creamy, mildly spicy vegetable soup is multi-purpose. It makes a wonderful warming first course, an appetizing quick meal and – when served chilled – is delicious for any summer menu.

INGREDIENTS

Serves 4–6
1 large potato, diced
1 small cauliflower, chopped
1 onion, chopped
15ml/1 tbsp oil
1 garlic clove, crushed
15ml/1 tbsp root ginger, grated
10ml/2 tsp ground turmeric
5ml/1 tsp cumin seeds
5ml/1 tsp black mustard seeds
10ml/2 tsp ground coriander
1 litre/1¾ pints/4 cups vegetable stock
300ml/½ pint/1¼ cups natural (plain)
    low fat yogurt
salt and black pepper
fresh coriander (cilantro) or parsley,
    to garnish

NUTRITIONAL NOTES	
Per Portion (4)	
Energy	188Kcals/789KJ
Fat	5.40g
Saturated Fat	0.77g
Carbohydrate	24.60g
Fibre	3.00g

—————— COOK'S TIP ——————

To make home-made vegetable stock, add to 3.5 litres/6 pints/15 cups of water, 2 sliced leeks, 3 sticks of chopped celery, 1 chopped onion, 1 chopped parsnip, 1 seeded and chopped yellow (bell) pepper, 3 crushed cloves of garlic, fresh herbs and seasoning of your choice and 45ml/3 tbsp light soy sauce. Slowly bring to the boil, then lower the heat and simmer for 30 minutes, stirring from time to time. Allow to cool. Strain, discard the vegetables, and use the stock as indicated in the recipe.

1 Put the potato, cauliflower and onion into a large heavy pan with the oil and 45ml/3 tbsp water. Heat until hot and bubbling, then cover and turn the heat down. Continue cooking the mixture for about 10 minutes.

2 Add the garlic, ginger and spices. Stir well, and cook for another 2 minutes, stirring occasionally. Pour in the stock and season well. Bring to the boil, then cover and simmer for about 20 minutes. Stir in the yogurt, adjust the seasoning, and serve garnished with coriander or parsley.

Chicken Naan Pockets

This quick-and-easy dish is ideal for a light snack lunch or supper. For speed, use the ready-to-bake naans available in most of today's supermarkets and Asian stores, but beware that as they are larger they will contain more fat.

INGREDIENTS

Serves 4
4 small naan, about 90g/3½oz each
45ml/3 tbsp natural (plain) low fat
  yogurt
7.5ml/1½ tsp garam masala
5ml/1 tsp chilli powder
5ml/1 tsp salt
45ml/3 tbsp lemon juice
15ml/1 tbsp chopped fresh coriander
  (cilantro)
1 green chilli, chopped
450g/1lb boneless chicken, skinned
  and cubed
8 onion rings
2 tomatoes, quartered
½ white cabbage, shredded

For the garnish
mixed salad leaves
2 small tomatoes, halved
lemon wedges
fresh coriander (cilantro)

NUTRITIONAL NOTES	
Per Portion	
Energy	472Kcals/1986KJ
Fat	15.30g
Saturated Fat	6.46g
Carbohydrate	53.40g
Fibre	4.20g

―――― COOK'S TIP ――――

For an even lower fat version, substitute wholemeal (whole-wheat) or plain pitta bread for the naan. Warm the pitta in the oven, split to form a pocket and then follow the recipe from step 2.

1 Cut into the middle of each naan to make a pocket, then set aside.

2 Mix together the yogurt, garam masala, chilli powder, salt, lemon juice, fresh coriander and green chilli. Pour the marinade over the chicken and leave to marinate for about 1 hour.

3 Preheat the grill (broiler) to very hot, then lower to medium. Put the chicken in a grill pan or flameproof dish lined with foil. Grill (broil) for 15–20 minutes until tender and cooked through, turning the chicken pieces at least twice.

4 Remove from the heat and fill each naan with the chicken and then with the onion rings, tomatoes and cabbage. Serve garnished with mixed salad leaves, tomato halves, lemon wedges and coriander.

Chicken Tikka

This extremely popular Indian appetizer is quick and easy to cook. The dish can also be served as a main course for four.

INGREDIENTS

Serves 6 as an appetizer

450g/1lb chicken fillets, skinned and cubed
5ml/1 tsp crushed fresh root ginger
5ml/1 tsp crushed garlic
5ml/1 tsp chilli powder
1.5ml/¼ tsp ground turmeric
5ml/1 tsp salt
150ml/¼ pint/⅔ cup natural (plain) low fat yogurt
60ml/4 tbsp lemon juice
15ml/1 tbsp fresh coriander (cilantro), chopped
15ml/1 tbsp oil

For the garnish
mixed salad leaves
1 small onion, cut into rings
lime wedges
fresh coriander (cilantro)

NUTRITIONAL NOTES	
Per Portion	
Energy	134Kcals/561KJ
Fat	5.50g
Saturated Fat	1.49g
Carbohydrate	3.90g
Fibre	0.30g

—————— COOK'S TIP ——————

To make the turning and basting of the chicken easier, thread the chicken pieces on to six wooden skewers before placing under the grill (broiler).

1 In a medium bowl, mix together the chicken pieces, ginger, garlic, chilli powder, turmeric, salt, yogurt, lemon juice and fresh coriander and leave to marinate for at least 2 hours.

3 Preheat the grill (broiler) to medium. Grill (broil) the chicken for 15–20 minutes until cooked, turning and basting several times. Serve on a bed of mixed salad leaves, garnished with onion rings, lime wedges and coriander.

2 Place in a grill pan or in a flameproof dish lined with foil and baste with the oil.

Vegetable Samosas

A selection of highly spiced vegetables in a pastry casing makes these samosas a delicious snack at any time of the day.

INGREDIENTS

Makes 28

14 sheets of filo pastry, thawed and
    wrapped in a damp dish towel
oil for brushing the pastries

For the filling

3 large potatoes, boiled and
    coarsely mashed
75g/3oz/¾ cup frozen peas, thawed
50g/2oz/⅓ cup canned corn, drained
5ml/1 tsp ground coriander
5ml/1 tsp ground cumin
5ml/1 tsp dry mango powder (*amchur*)
1 small onion, finely chopped
2 green chillies, finely chopped
30ml/2 tbsp coriander (cilantro) leaves,
    chopped
30ml/2 tbsp mint leaves, chopped
juice of 1 lemon
salt, to taste

NUTRITIONAL NOTES	
Per Samosa	
Energy	50Kcals/205KJ
Fat	0.78g
Saturated Fat	0.10g
Carbohydrate	9.40g
Fibre	0.50g

1 Preheat the oven to 200°C/400°F/ Gas 6. Cut each sheet of filo pastry in half lengthways and fold each piece in half lengthways to give 28 thin strips. Lightly brush with oil.

--- COOK'S TIP ---

Work with one or two sheets of filo pastry at a time and keep the rest covered with a damp dish towel to prevent it drying out.

2 Toss all the filling ingredients together in a large mixing bowl until they are well blended. Adjust the seasoning with salt and lemon juice if necessary.

3 Using one strip of the pastry at a time, place 15ml/1 tbsp of the filling mixture at one end of the strip and diagonally fold the pastry up to form a triangle shape. Brush the samosas with oil and bake in the oven for 10–15 minutes, until golden brown.

Tandoori Masala Spring Lamb Chops

These spicy, lean and trimmed lamb chops are marinated for three hours and then cooked in the oven using very little oil. They make an excellent appetizer, served with a salad garnish, and would also serve three as a main course with rice.

INGREDIENTS

Serves 6 as an appetizer
6 small lean spring lamb chops
30ml/2 tbsp natural (plain) low fat
    yogurt
15ml/1 tbsp tomato purée (paste)
10ml/2 tsp ground coriander
5ml/1 tsp crushed fresh root ginger
5ml/1 tsp crushed garlic
5ml/1 tsp chilli powder
few drops of red food colouring
    (optional)
5ml/1 tsp salt
15ml/1 tbsp oil, plus extra
    for basting
45ml/3 tbsp lemon juice

For the salad garnish
lettuce leaves (optional)
lime wedges
1 small onion, sliced
fresh coriander (cilantro)

NUTRITIONAL NOTES	
Per Portion	
Energy	117Kcals/488KJ
Fat	6.60g
Saturated Fat	2.42g
Carbohydrate	3.10g
Fibre	0.30g

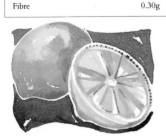

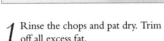

1 Rinse the chops and pat dry. Trim off all excess fat.

2 In a medium bowl, mix together the yogurt, tomato purée, ground coriander, ginger and crushed garlic, chilli powder, food colouring (if using), salt, oil and lemon juice.

3 Rub this spice mixture over the lamb chops, using your hands, and leave the chops to marinate in a cool place for at least 3 hours.

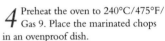

4 Preheat the oven to 240°C/475°F/ Gas 9. Place the marinated chops in an ovenproof dish.

5 Using a brush, baste the chops with about 5ml/1 tsp oil and cook in the oven for 15 minutes. Lower the heat to 180°C/350°F/Gas 4 and cook for a further 10–15 minutes.

6 Check that the chops are cooked and serve immediately on a bed of lettuce leaves, if wished, and garnish with lime wedges, sliced onion and fresh coriander.

_____ COOK'S TIP _____

This bright red tandoori masala mixture is used to colour and spice both meat and chicken and give the effect of a tandoori-style dish without the need to cook it in a traditional clay oven (*tandoor*).

Prawns with Vegetables

This light and nutritious appetizer is excellent served on a bed of lettuce leaves. Alternatively, serve the prawns (shrimp) with some plain boiled rice for a quick lunch or with a selection of vegetable dishes for a main course meal.

INGREDIENTS

Serves 4

30ml/2 tbsp fresh coriander (cilantro), chopped
5ml/1 tsp salt
2 green chillies
45ml/3 tbsp lemon juice
30ml/2 tbsp oil
20 cooked king prawns (jumbo shrimp), peeled
1 medium courgette (zucchini), thickly sliced
1 medium onion, cut into 8 chunks
8 cherry tomatoes
8 baby corn on the cobs
mixed salad leaves, to serve

NUTRITIONAL NOTES	
Per Portion	
Energy	183Kcals/767KJ
Fat	7.70g
Saturated Fat	1.04g
Carbohydrate	4.50g
Fibre	1.30g

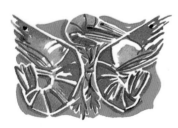

1 Place the chopped coriander, salt, chillies, lemon juice and oil in a food processor and grind these together for a few seconds.

2 Remove the spice paste from the food processor and transfer to a medium mixing bowl.

3 Add the peeled prawns to the spices and stir to make sure that all the prawns are well coated. Set aside to marinate for about 30 minutes.

4 Preheat the grill (broiler) to very hot, then turn down to medium.

5 Arrange the vegetables and prawns alternately on 4 skewers. When all the skewers are ready, place them under the grill for 5–7 minutes until cooked and browned.

6 Serve immediately on a bed of mixed salad leaves.

_____ COOK'S TIP _____

King prawns are a luxury, but well worth choosing for a special dinner. For a more economical variation, substitute the king prawns (jumbo shrimp) with 450g/1lb ordinary prawns (shrimp).

Pineapple Chicken Kebabs

This chicken dish has a delicate tang and the meat is very tender. The pineapple not only tenderizes the chicken but also gives it a slight sweetness.

INGREDIENTS

Serves 6

225g/8oz/1 cup canned pineapple chunks
5ml/1 tsp ground cumin
5ml/1 tsp ground coriander
5ml/1 tsp chilli powder
2.5ml/½ tsp crushed garlic
5ml/1 tsp salt
30ml/2 tbsp natural (plain) low fat yogurt
15ml/1 tbsp chopped fresh coriander (cilantro)
few drops of orange food colouring
275g/10oz chicken fillets, skinned
½ red (bell) pepper, seeded
½ yellow or green (bell) pepper, seeded
1 large onion
6 cherry tomatoes
15ml/1 tbsp oil
salad leaves, to serve

NUTRITIONAL NOTES	
Per Portion	
Energy	183Kcals/768KJ
Fat	6.60g
Saturated Fat	1.47g
Carbohydrate	15.40g
Fibre	1.80g

_____ COOK'S TIP _____

If possible, use a mixture of chicken breast fillets and thigh meat for this recipe.

1 Drain the pineapple juice into a bowl. Reserve 8 large chunks of pineapple and squeeze the juice from the remaining chunks into the bowl and set aside. You should have about 120ml/4fl oz/½ cup pineapple juice.

2 In a large bowl, blend together the spices, garlic, salt, yogurt, fresh coriander and food colouring. Mix in the reserved pineapple juice.

3 Cut the chicken into bitesize cubes, add to the yogurt and spice mixture and leave to marinate in a cool place for about 1–1½ hours.

4 Cut the peppers and onion into bitesize chunks.

5 Preheat the grill (broiler) to medium. Arrange the chicken pieces, vegetables and reserved pineapple chunks alternately on 6 wooden or metal skewers.

6 Brush the kebabs lightly with the oil, then place the skewers on a flameproof dish or in a grill pan, turning the chicken pieces and basting with the marinade regularly, for about 15 minutes until cooked through. Serve with salad leaves.

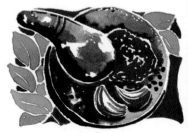

Spicy Pepper Soup

This is a highly soothing broth for winter evenings, also known as *Mulla-ga-tani*. Serve with the whole spices, or strain and reheat if you prefer. The lemon juice may be adjusted to taste, but this dish should be distinctly sour.

INGREDIENTS

Serves 4

30ml/2 tbsp vegetable oil
2.5ml/½ tsp pepper, ground black
5ml/1 tsp cumin seeds
2.5 ml/½ tsp mustard seeds
1.5ml/¼ tsp asafoetida
2 whole dried red chillies
4–6 curry leaves
2.5ml/½ tsp ground turmeric
2 garlic cloves, crushed
300ml/½ pint/1¼ cups tomato juice
juice of 2 lemons
120ml/4fl oz/½ cup water
salt, to taste
coriander (cilantro) leaves, chopped, to garnish

NUTRITIONAL NOTES	
Per Portion	
Energy	100Kcals/413KJ
Fat	8.10g
Saturated Fat	0.88g
Carbohydrate	5.20g
Fibre	0.60g

_____ COOK'S TIP _____

Don't be put off by the unpleasant smell of asafoetida as it disappears when cooked. Used in small quantities, as here, asafoetida adds an oniony flavour to foods.

_____ VARIATION _____

For a slightly more bitter flavour, use lime juice instead of lemon juice. Add 5ml/1 tsp tamarind paste for extra sourness.

1 In a heavy pan, heat the oil and fry the pepper, cumin and mustard seeds, asafoetida, chillies, curry leaves, turmeric and garlic until the chillies are nearly black and the garlic is golden brown.

2 Lower the heat and add the tomato juice, lemon juice, water and salt. Bring the soup to the boil, then lower the heat and simmer gently for about 10 minutes. Pour the soup into bowls, garnish with the chopped coriander and serve immediately.

Spicy Yogurt Soup

INGREDIENTS

Serves 4

450ml/³/₄ pint/1½ cups natural (plain)
    low fat yogurt, beaten
60ml/4 tbsp gram flour
2.5ml/½ tsp chilli powder
2.5ml/½ tsp ground turmeric
salt, to taste
2–3 green chillies, finely chopped
30ml/2 tbsp vegetable oil
4 whole dried red chillies
5ml/1 tsp cumin seeds
3–4 curry leaves
3 garlic cloves, crushed
5cm/2in piece of fresh root
    ginger, crushed
fresh coriander (cilantro) leaves,
    chopped, to garnish

NUTRITIONAL NOTES	
Per Portion (4)	
Energy	196Kcals/820KJ
Fat	9.70g
Saturated Fat	1.49g
Carbohydrate	18.30g
Fibre	1.80g

1 Mix together the yogurt, gram
flour, chilli powder, turmeric and
salt and pass them through a strainer
into a pan. Add the green chillies and
cook gently for about 10 minutes,
stirring occasionally. Be careful not to
let the soup boil over.

2 Heat the oil in a heavy pan and fry
the remaining spices, crushed
garlic and fresh ginger until the dried
chillies turn black.

_____ COOK'S TIP _____

For a lower fat version drain off some of
the oil before adding it to the yogurt.
Adjust the amount of chillies according to
how hot you want the soup to be.

3 Pour the oil and the spices over the
yogurt soup, cover the pan and
leave to rest for 5 minutes off the heat.
Mix well and gently reheat for a further
5 minutes. Serve hot, garnished with
the coriander leaves.

Ginger Chicken Wings

INGREDIENTS

Serves 4

10–12 chicken wings, skinned
175ml/6fl oz/³⁄₄ cup natural (plain)
　low fat yogurt
7.5ml/1½ tsp crushed fresh root ginger
5ml/1 tsp salt
5ml/1 tsp Tabasco sauce
15ml/1 tbsp tomato ketchup
5ml/1 tsp crushed garlic
15ml/1 tbsp lemon juice
15ml/1 tbsp coriander (cilantro) leaves
15ml/1 tbsp oil
2 medium onions, sliced
15ml/1 tbsp shredded root ginger

NUTRITIONAL NOTES	
Per Portion	
Energy	224Kcals/936KJ
Fat	9.00g
Saturated Fat	2.23g
Carbohydrate	12.64g
Fibre	1.24g

1 Place the chicken wings in a glass or china bowl. Pour the yogurt into a separate bowl along with the ginger pulp, salt, Tabasco sauce, tomato ketchup, garlic pulp, lemon juice and half the fresh coriander leaves. Whisk everything together, then pour the mixture over the chicken wings and stir gently to coat the chicken.

2 Heat the oil in a wok or heavy frying pan and fry the onions until soft.

3 Pour in the chicken wings and cook over medium heat, stirring occasionally, for 10–15 minutes.

4 Add the remaining coriander and the shredded ginger and serve hot.

___ COOK'S TIP ___

You can substitute drumsticks or other chicken portions for the wings in this recipe, but remember to increase the cooking time.

Glazed Garlic Shrimp

It is best to peel the prawns for this dish as it helps them to absorb maximum flavour. Serve with salad as an appetizer or with rice and accompaniments for a more substantial meal.

INGREDIENTS

Serves 4

15ml/1 tbsp oil
3 garlic cloves, roughly chopped
3 tomatoes, chopped
2.5ml/½ tsp salt
5ml/1 tsp crushed red chillies
5ml/1 tsp lemon juice
15ml/1 tbsp mango chutney
1 fresh green chilli, chopped
15–20 cooked king prawns (jumbo shrimp), peeled
fresh coriander (cilantro), to garnish

NUTRITIONAL NOTES	
Per Portion	
Energy	73Kcals/302KJ
Fat	3.30g
Saturated Fat	0.38g
Carbohydrate	4.90g
Fibre	0.80g

1 In a pan, heat the oil and add the garlic. Cook gently for 2 minutes.

_____ COOK'S TIP _____

Use a skewer or the point of a knife to remove the black intestinal vein running down the back of the prawns.

2 Lower the heat and add the chopped tomatoes to the pan along with the salt, crushed red chillies, lemon juice, mango chutney and fresh green chilli.

3 Finally, add the prawns, turn up the heat and stir-fry these quickly, until heated through.

4 Transfer the prawns to a serving dish. Serve garnished with fresh coriander sprigs.

MEAT DISHES

Although lamb has a high fat content, you can still enjoy traditional favourites such as Creamy Lamb Korma and Lamb Meatballs if you choose tastier spring lamb and remove all the excess fat before you start cooking. Other recipes adapted for low fat eating in this section include Beef Madras and Beef Vindaloo.

Lamb with Peas and Mint

A simple minced lamb dish, this is easy to prepare and very versatile. It is equally delicious whether served with plain boiled rice or chappatis.

INGREDIENTS

Serves 4

15ml/1 tbsp oil
1 medium onion, chopped
2.5ml/½ tsp crushed garlic
2.5ml/½ tsp crushed fresh root ginger
2.5ml/½ tsp chilli powder
1.5ml/¼ tsp ground turmeric
5ml/1 tsp ground coriander
5ml/1 tsp salt
2 medium tomatoes, sliced
275g/10oz lean leg of lamb, minced (ground)
1 large carrot, sliced or cut into batons
75g/3oz/½ cup petit pois (baby peas)
15ml/1 tbsp chopped fresh mint
15ml/1 tbsp chopped fresh coriander (cilantro)
1 green chilli, chopped
fresh coriander (cilantro), to garnish

NUTRITIONAL NOTES	
Per Portion	
Energy	178Kcals/742KJ
Fat	9.40g
Saturated Fat	3.32g
Carbohydrate	7.20g
Fibre	2.10g

—————— COOK'S TIP ——————

To cut the carrot into batons, first cut it into 5cm/2in lengths and square up the sides. Slice the carrot lengthways, then cut the pieces again at the identical width to make strips.

1 In a deep frying pan, heat the oil and fry the chopped onion over medium heat for 5 minutes until golden in colour.

2 Meanwhile, in a small mixing bowl, blend together the garlic, ginger, chilli powder, turmeric, ground coriander and salt.

3 Add the sliced tomatoes and the spice mixture to the onions in the frying pan and fry for 2–3 minutes, stirring continuously.

4 Add the minced lamb to the mixture and stir-fry for about 7–10 minutes to seal.

5 Break up any lumps of meat which may form in the pan, using a potato masher if necessary.

6 Finally add the carrot, petit pois, chopped fresh mint and coriander and the chopped green chilli and mix together well.

7 Stir-fry for another 2–3 minutes until the carrot slices or batons and the petit pois are cooked, then serve immediately, garnished with fresh coriander sprigs.

Balti Keema with Curry Leaves and Chillies

Minced (ground) lamb is cooked in its own juices with a few spices and herbs, but no other liquid.

Ingredients

Serves 4

10ml/2 tsp oil
2 medium onions, chopped
10 curry leaves
6 green chillies
350g/12oz lean minced (ground) lamb
5ml/1 tsp crushed garlic
5ml/1 tsp crushed fresh root ginger
5ml/1 tsp chilli powder
1.5ml/¼ tsp ground turmeric
5ml/1 tsp salt
2 tomatoes, peeled and quartered
15ml/1 tbsp chopped fresh coriander
   (cilantro)

1 Heat the oil in a wok or frying pan and fry the onions together with the curry leaves and 3 of the whole green chillies.

2 Put the lamb into a bowl and blend thoroughly with the garlic, ginger, chilli powder, turmeric and salt.

_____ Cook's Tip _____

This curry also makes a terrific brunch if served with fried eggs.

3 Add the lamb to the onions and stir-fry for 7–10 minutes.

4 Add the tomatoes, coriander and chillies and stir-fry for 2 minutes.

Nutritional Notes	
Per Portion	
Energy	197Kcals/821KJ
Fat	9.37g
Saturated Fat	3.59g
Carbohydrate	8.57g
Fibre	1.63g

Lamb with Apricots

Lamb is combined with apricots and traditional Indian spices to produce a rich, spicy curry with a hint of sweetness.

INGREDIENTS

Serves 6

900g/2lb lean stewing lamb
15ml/1 tbsp oil
2.5cm/1in cinnamon stick
4 green cardamom pods
1 onion, chopped
15ml/1 tbsp curry paste
5ml/1 tsp ground cumin
5ml/1 tsp ground coriander
1.5ml/¼ tsp salt
175g/6oz ready-to-eat dried apricots
350ml/12fl oz/1½ cups lamb stock
fresh coriander (cilantro), to garnish
yellow rice and mango chutney,
    to serve

1 Remove all the fat from the lamb and cut into 2.5cm/1in cubes.

NUTRITIONAL NOTES	
Per Portion	
Energy	327Kcals/1368KJ
Fat	16.00g
Saturated Fat	6.59g
Carbohydrate	13.30g
Fibre	2.70g

2 Heat the oil in a large pan and fry the cinnamon stick and cardamoms for 2 minutes. Add the onion and gently fry for about 6–8 minutes, stirring occasionally.

3 Add the curry paste and fry for 2 minutes. Stir in the cumin, coriander and salt and stir-fry for a further 2–3 minutes.

4 Add the meat, apricots and the stock. Cover and cook for 1–1½ hours. Serve, garnished with fresh coriander, on yellow rice, with the chutney in a separate bowl.

Stir-fried Lamb with Baby Onions and Peppers

The baby onions are used whole in this recipe. Serve this dish with rice or lentils.

INGREDIENTS

Serves 4

15ml/1 tbsp oil
8 baby (pearl) onions
225g/8oz boned lean lamb, cut
   into strips
5ml/1 tsp ground cumin
5ml/1 tsp ground coriander
15ml/1 tbsp tomato purée (paste)
5ml/1 tsp chilli powder
5ml/1 tsp salt
15ml/1 tbsp lemon juice
2.5ml/½ tsp onion seeds
4 curry leaves
300ml/½ pint/1¼ cups water
1 small red (bell) pepper, seeded and
   roughly sliced
1 small green (bell) pepper, seeded and
   roughly sliced
15ml/1 tbsp chopped fresh coriander
   (cilantro)
15ml/1 tbsp chopped fresh mint

1 Heat the oil in a wok or frying pan and stir-fry the whole baby onions for about 3 minutes. Using a slotted spoon, remove the onions from the wok and set aside to drain.

2 Mix together the lamb, cumin, ground coriander, tomato purée, chilli powder, salt and lemon juice in a bowl and set aside.

3 Reheat the oil and briskly stir-fry the onion seeds and curry leaves for 2–3 minutes.

--- COOK'S TIP ---

This dish benefits from being cooked a day in advance and kept in the refrigerator overnight, making it an ideal dish to serve for a relaxed dinner party.

NUTRITIONAL NOTES	
Per Portion	
Energy	155Kcals/644KJ
Fat	9.48g
Saturated Fat	2.82g
Carbohydrate	5.74g
Fibre	1.49g

4 Add the lamb and spice mixture and stir-fry for about 5 minutes, then pour in the water, lower the heat and cook gently for about 10 minutes, until the lamb is cooked through.

5 Add the peppers and half the fresh coriander and mint. Stir-fry for a further 2 minutes.

6 Finally, add the baby onions and the remaining chopped fresh coriander and mint and serve.

Lamb Meatballs

INGREDIENTS

Serves 6

For the meatballs

675g/1½lb lean minced (ground) lamb
1 green chilli, roughly chopped
1 garlic clove, chopped
2.5cm/1in piece root ginger, chopped
1.5ml/¼ tsp garam masala
1.5ml/¼ tsp salt
45ml/3 tbsp chopped fresh coriander
   (cilantro), plus extra to garnish
pilau rice, to serve

For the sauce

15ml/1 tbsp oil
2.5ml/½ tsp cumin seeds
1 onion, chopped
1 garlic clove, chopped
2.5cm/1in piece root ginger,
   finely chopped
5ml/1 tsp ground cumin
5ml/1 tsp ground coriander
2.5ml/½ tsp salt
2.5ml/½ tsp chilli powder
15ml/1 tbsp tomato purée (paste)
400g/14oz can chopped tomatoes

NUTRITIONAL NOTES	
Per Portion	
Energy	231Kcals/968KJ
Fat	12.30g
Saturated Fat	5.00g
Carbohydrate	5.40g
Fibre	0.90g

1 To make the meatballs, put all the ingredients into a food processor or blender and process until the mixture binds together.

2 Shape the mixture into 18 balls. Cover and chill for 10 minutes.

3 To make the sauce, heat the oil in a pan and fry the cumin seeds until they splutter. Add the onion, garlic and ginger and fry for 5 minutes. Stir in the remaining sauce ingredients and simmer for 5 minutes.

4 Add the meatballs to the sauce. Bring to the boil, cover and simmer for 25–30 minutes or until the meatballs are cooked through. Serve on a bed of pilau rice and garnish with the extra fresh coriander.

_____ COOK'S TIP _____

You can make the meatballs a day in advance. Cover with clear film (plastic wrap) and store in the refrigerator until needed.

Lamb Kebabs

First introduced by the Muslims, kebabs have now become a favourite Indian dish.

INGREDIENTS

Serves 8
For the kebabs
900g/2lb lean minced (ground) lamb
1 large onion, roughly chopped
5cm/2in piece root ginger, chopped
2 garlic cloves, crushed
1 green chilli, finely chopped
5ml/1 tsp chilli powder
30ml/2 tbsp chopped fresh coriander
   (cilantro)
5ml/1 tsp garam masala
10ml/2 tsp ground coriander
5ml/1 tsp ground cumin
5ml/1 tsp salt
1 egg
15ml/1 tbsp natural (plain) low fat
   yogurt
15ml/1 tbsp oil
mixed salad, to serve

For the raita
250ml/8fl oz/1 cup natural (plain)
   low fat yogurt
½ cucumber, finely chopped
30ml/2 tbsp chopped fresh mint
1.5ml/¼ tsp salt

1 Put all the ingredients for the kebabs, except the yogurt and oil, into a food processor or blender and process until the mixture binds together. Spoon into a bowl and leave to marinate for 1 hour.

2 For the raita, mix together all the ingredients and chill for at least 15 minutes in a refrigerator.

3 Preheat the grill (broiler). Divide the lamb mixture into eight equal portions with lightly floured hands and shape into long sausages. Thread on to skewers and chill.

4 Brush the kebabs lightly with the yogurt and oil and cook under a hot grill (broiler) for 8–10 minutes, turning occasionally, until brown all over. Serve the kebabs on a bed of mixed salad accompanied by the raita.

NUTRITIONAL NOTES	
Per Portion	
Energy	249Kcals/1045KJ
Fat	12.75g
Saturated Fat	5.30g
Carbohydrate	7.00g
Fibre	0.60g

Courgettes with Lamb

Lamb is cooked with yogurt and then the sliced courgettes, which have already been grilled, are added to the mixture.

INGREDIENTS

Serves 4

15ml/1 tbsp oil
2 medium onions, chopped
225g/8oz lean lamb steaks, cut
  into strips
120ml/4fl oz/½ cup natural (plain)
  low fat yogurt
5ml/1 tsp garam masala
5ml/1 tsp chilli powder
5ml/1 tsp crushed garlic
5ml/1 tsp crushed fresh root ginger
2.5ml/½ tsp ground coriander
2 medium courgettes (zucchini), sliced
15ml/1 tbsp chopped fresh coriander
  (cilantro), to garnish

NUTRITIONAL NOTES	
Per Portion	
Energy	178Kcals/742KJ
Fat	8.36g
Saturated Fat	2.78g
Carbohydrate	10.83g
Fibre	1.99g

--- COOK'S TIP ---

Frying onions in very little oil needs to be done over a low heat and requires some patience. They will take a little longer to brown and should be gently stirred only occasionally. Excessive stirring will draw the moisture out of the onions and make them even more difficult to fry.

1 Heat the oil in a wok or frying pan and fry the onions until golden brown.

2 Add the lamb strips and stir-fry for 1 minute to seal the meat.

3 Put the yogurt, garam masala, chilli powder, garlic, ginger and ground coriander into a bowl. Whisk the mixture together.

4 Pour the yogurt mixture over the lamb and stir-fry for 2 minutes. Cover and cook over medium to low heat for 12–15 minutes.

5 Put the courgettes in a dish and cook under a preheated grill (broiler) for about 3 minutes, turning once.

6 Check that the lamb is cooked through and the sauce is quite thick, then add the courgettes and serve garnished with the fresh coriander.

Balti Lamb with Cauliflower

Cauliflower and lamb go beautifully together. This curry is given a final *tarka*, a seasoned oil, of cumin seeds and curry leaves, to enhance the flavour.

INGREDIENTS

Serves 4

10ml/2 tsp oil
2 medium onions, sliced
7.5ml/1½ tsp crushed fresh root ginger
5ml/1 tsp chilli powder
5ml/1 tsp crushed garlic
1.5ml/¼ tsp ground turmeric
2.5ml/½ tsp ground coriander
30ml/2 tbsp fresh fenugreek leaves
275g/10oz boned lean spring lamb, cut into strips
1 small cauliflower, cut into small florets
300ml/½ pint/1¼ cups water
30ml/2 tbsp fresh coriander (cilantro) leaves
½ red (bell) pepper, seeded and sliced
15ml/1 tbsp lemon juice

For the *tarka*

10ml/2 tsp oil
2.5ml/½ tsp cumin seeds
4–6 curry leaves

1 Heat the oil in a wok or a frying pan and gently fry the onions until they are golden brown. Lower the heat and then add the crushed fresh root ginger, chilli powder, crushed garlic, turmeric and ground coriander. Stir well to combine all the ingredients, then add the fresh fenugreek leaves.

2 Add the lamb strips to the wok and stir-fry until the lamb is completely coated with the spices. Add half the cauliflower florets and stir the mixture well.

3 Pour in the water, cover the wok, lower the heat and cook for 5–7 minutes until the cauliflower and lamb are almost cooked through.

4 Add the remaining cauliflower, half the fresh coriander, the red pepper and lemon juice and stir-fry for about 5 minutes, ensuring the sauce does not catch on the bottom of the wok.

5 Check that the lamb is completely cooked, then remove from the heat and set aside.

6 To make the *tarka*, heat the oil and fry the seeds and curry leaves for about 30 seconds. While it is still hot, pour the seasoned oil over the cauliflower and lamb and serve garnished with the remaining fresh coriander leaves.

NUTRITIONAL NOTES	
Per Portion	
Energy	202Kcals/839KJ
Fat	9.88g
Saturated Fat	3.24g
Carbohydrate	10.86g
Fibre	2.88g

_____ COOK'S TIP _____

Groundnut (peanut) oil is an excellent oil to use for curries.

Spicy Lamb and Potato Stew

Transform this simple dish into a
tasty stew with the addition of
Indian spices.

INGREDIENTS

Serves 6

675g/1½lb lean lamb fillet
15ml/1 tbsp oil
1 onion, finely chopped
2 bay leaves
1 green chilli, seeded and finely chopped
2 garlic cloves, finely chopped
10ml/2 tsp ground coriander
5ml/1 tsp ground cumin
2.5ml/½ tsp ground turmeric
2.5ml/½ tsp chilli powder
2.5ml/½ tsp salt
225g/8oz tomatoes, peeled and
    finely chopped
600ml/1 pint/2½ cups chicken stock
2 large potatoes, cut into
    2.5cm/1in chunks
chopped fresh coriander (cilantro),
    to garnish

NUTRITIONAL NOTES	
Per Portion	
Energy	283Kcals/1187KJ
Fat	12.40g
Saturated Fat	5.02g
Carbohydrate	17.20g
Fibre	1.70g

1 Remove any visible fat from the
lamb and cut the meat into
2.5cm/1in cubes.

2 Heat the oil in a large pan and fry
the onion, bay leaves, chilli and
garlic for 5 minutes.

3 Add the meat and cook for about
6–8 minutes until lightly browned.

4 Add the ground coriander, ground
cumin, ground turmeric, chilli
powder and salt and cook the spices for
3–4 minutes, stirring all the time to
prevent the spices from sticking to the
bottom of the pan.

5 Add the tomatoes and stock and
simmer for 5 minutes until the
sauce thickens. Bring to the boil, cover
and simmer for 1 hour.

6 Add the potatoes and cook for a
further 30–40 minutes or until the
meat is tender. Garnish with chopped
fresh coriander and serve.

_____ COOK'S TIP _____

This stew is absolutely delicious served
with warm, freshly made chappatis.

Mini Mince Koftas in a Spicy Sauce

This kofta curry is very popular in most Indian homes. It is also extremely easy to make. Serve with plain boiled pilau rice.

Ingredients

Serves 4

225g/8oz lean minced (ground) lamb
10ml/2 tsp poppy seeds
1 medium onion, chopped
5ml/1 tsp crushed fresh root ginger
5ml/1 tsp crushed garlic
5ml/1 tsp salt
5ml/1 tsp chilli powder
7.5ml/1½ tsp ground coriander
30ml/2 tbsp fresh coriander (cilantro) leaves
1 small egg

For the sauce

85ml/3fl oz/⅓ cup natural (plain) low fat yogurt
30ml/2 tbsp tomato purée (paste)
5ml/1 tsp chilli powder
5ml/1 tsp salt
5ml/1 tsp crushed garlic
5ml/1 tsp crushed fresh root ginger
5ml/1 tsp garam masala
10ml/2 tsp oil
1 cinnamon stick
400ml/14fl oz/1⅔ cups water

1 Place the minced lamb in a food processor and mince (grind) it further for about 1 minute. Remove from the processor, put in a bowl, tip the poppy seeds on top and set aside.

2 Place the onion in the food processor, together with the crushed fresh root ginger, crushed garlic, salt, chilli powder, ground coriander and half the fresh coriander. Grind this spice mixture for about 30 seconds, then blend it into the minced lamb.

3 Whisk the egg and thoroughly mix it into the minced lamb. Leave to stand for about 1 hour.

4 For the sauce, whisk together the yogurt, tomato purée, chilli powder, salt, crushed garlic, crushed fresh root ginger and garam masala.

5 Heat the oil with the cinnamon stick in a wok or frying pan for about 1 minute, then pour in the prepared sauce. Lower the heat and cook for about 1 minute. Remove the wok or frying pan from the heat and set aside.

6 Break off small balls of the mince mixture and make the koftas using your hands. When all the koftas are ready, return the sauce to the heat and add the water. Drop in the koftas one by one. Place the remaining fresh coriander on top, cover with a lid and cook for 7–10 minutes, stirring gently now and again to turn the koftas around. Serve hot.

Nutritional Notes	
Per Portion	
Energy	155Kcals/647KJ
Fat	9.24g
Saturated Fat	2.79g
Carbohydrate	7.56g
Fibre	1.16g

Balti Bhoona Lamb

Bhooning is a very traditional way of stir-frying which simply involves semi-circular movements, scraping the bottom of the wok each time in the middle. Serve this dish with a freshly made chappati.

INGREDIENTS

Serves 4

225–275g/8–10oz boned lean
   spring lamb
3 medium onions
15ml/1 tbsp oil
15ml/1 tbsp tomato purée (paste)
5ml/1 tsp crushed garlic
7.5ml/1½ tsp crushed fresh root ginger
5ml/1 tsp salt
1.5ml/¼ tsp ground turmeric
600ml/1 pint/2½ cups water
15ml/1 tbsp lemon juice
15ml/1 tbsp shredded fresh root ginger
15ml/1 tbsp chopped fresh coriander
   (cilantro)
15ml/1 tbsp chopped fresh mint
1 red chilli, chopped

1 Using a sharp knife remove any excess fat from the lamb and cut the meat into small cubes.

COOK'S TIP

Bhooning ensures that the meat becomes well-coated and combined with the spice mixture before the cooking liquid is added.

2 Dice the onions finely. Heat the oil in a wok or frying pan and fry the onions until soft.

3 Meanwhile, mix together the tomato purée, garlic and ginger pulp, salt and turmeric. Pour the spice mixture on to the onions in the wok and stir-fry for a few seconds.

4 Add the lamb and continue to stir-fry for about 2–3 minutes. Stir in the water, lower the heat, cover the wok and cook for 15–20 minutes, stirring occasionally.

5 When the water has almost evaporated, start bhooning over a medium heat (see the introduction above), making sure that the sauce does not catch on the bottom of the wok. Continue for 5–7 minutes.

6 Pour in the lemon juice, followed by the shredded ginger, coriander, mint and red chilli, then serve.

NUTRITIONAL NOTES	
Per Portion	
Energy	198Kcals/825KJ
Fat	10.37g
Saturated Fat	3.24g
Carbohydrate	11.05g
Fibre	1.84g

Khara Masala Lamb

This is another dish which involves bhooning – stirring with a semi-circular motion. Whole spices are used, so warn the diners of their presence in advance! This curry is delicious served with freshly baked naan bread or plain rice.

Ingredients

Serves 4

15ml/1 tbsp oil
2 onions, chopped
5ml/1 tsp shredded ginger
5ml/1 tsp sliced garlic
6 dried red chillies
3 cardamom pods
2 cinnamon sticks
6 black peppercorns
3 cloves
2.5ml/½ tsp salt
450g/1lb boned lean leg of lamb, cubed
600ml/1 pint/2½ cups water
2 fresh green chillies, sliced
30ml/2 tbsp chopped fresh coriander
  (cilantro)

Nutritional Notes	
Per Portion	
Energy	242Kcals/1012KJ
Fat	13.20g
Saturated Fat	5.19g
Carbohydrate	6.70g
Fibre	0.90g

_____ Cook's Tip _____

For a tasty alternative, instead of the boned leg of lamb used here, use the equivalent weight of either lean skinned chicken or beef cut into cubes.

1 Heat the oil in a large pan. Lower the heat and fry the onions until they are lightly browned, stirring occasionally.

2 Add half the ginger and half the garlic and stir well.

3 Throw in half the red chillies, the cardamom pods, cinnamon, peppercorns, cloves and salt.

4 Add the lamb and fry over medium heat. Stir continuously with a semi-circular movement, using a wooden spoon to scrape the bottom of the pan and prevent the meat from burning. Cook for about 5 minutes.

5 Pour in the water, cover with a lid and cook slowly over medium-low heat for 35–40 minutes, or until the water has evaporated and the meat is tender, stirring from time to time to prevent the mixture from burning on the bottom of the pan.

6 Add the rest of the shredded ginger and sliced garlic and the remaining dried red chillies, along with the sliced fresh green chillies and the chopped coriander.

7 Continue to stir the mixture over the heat until you see some free oil on the sides of the pan, then remove it from the heat. Transfer the curry to a serving dish and serve immediately.

Balti Spring Lamb Chops

INGREDIENTS

Serves 4

8 small lean spring lamb chops
1 large red chilli, seeded
30ml/2 tbsp chopped coriander (cilantro)
15ml/1 tbsp chopped fresh mint
5ml/1 tsp salt
5ml/1 tsp soft brown sugar
5ml/1 tsp garam masala
5ml/1 tsp crushed garlic
5ml/1 tsp crushed fresh root ginger
175ml/6fl oz/³/₄ cup low fat natural
   (plain) yogurt
10ml/2 tsp oil

NUTRITIONAL NOTES	
Per Portion	
Energy	207Kcals/864KJ
Fat	10.29g
Saturated Fat	4.26g
Carbohydrate	6.63g
Fibre	0.27g

1 Trim the lamb chops of any excess fat. Place them in a large bowl.

2 Finely chop the chilli, then mix together with the coriander, mint, salt, brown sugar, garam masala, crushed garlic and ginger.

3 Pour the yogurt into the herb mixture and, using a small whisk or a fork, mix together thoroughly. Pour this mixture over the top of the chops and turn them with your fingers to make sure that they are completely covered. Leave to marinate overnight in the refrigerator.

4 Heat the oil in a large wok or frying pan and add the chops. Cook over medium heat for about 20 minutes or until cooked right through, turning the chops from time to time. Alternatively, grill (broil) the chops, basting with oil throughout. Serve with a mixed salad.

Creamy Lamb Korma

Cutting the lamb into strips for this lovely dish makes it easier and quicker to cook.

INGREDIENTS

Serves 4

2 green chillies
120ml/4fl oz/½ cup natural (plain) low fat yogurt
50ml/2fl oz/¼ cup coconut milk
15ml/1 tbsp ground almonds
5ml/1 tsp salt
5ml/1 tsp crushed garlic
5ml/1 tsp crushed fresh root ginger
5ml/1 tsp garam masala
1.5ml/¼ tsp ground cardamom
large pinch of ground cinnamon
15ml/1 tbsp chopped fresh mint
15ml/1 tbsp oil
2 medium onions, diced
1 bay leaf
4 black peppercorns
225g/8oz lean lamb, cut into strips
150ml/¼ pint/⅔ cup water
fresh mint leaves, to garnish

2 Heat the oil in a wok or heavy frying pan and fry the onions with the bay leaf and peppercorns for about 5 minutes.

4 Pour in the yogurt mixture and water, lower the heat, cover and cook for about 15 minutes or until the lamb is cooked through, stirring occasionally. Stir-fry for a further 2 minutes. Serve garnished with fresh mint leaves.

COOK'S TIP

Rice with Peas and Curry Leaves goes very well with this korma.

3 When the onions are soft and golden brown, add the lamb and stir-fry for about 2 minutes.

1 Finely chop the chillies. Whisk the yogurt with the chillies, coconut milk, ground almonds, salt, garlic, ginger, garam masala, cardamom, cinnamon and mint.

NUTRITIONAL NOTES	
Per Portion	
Energy	193Kcals/803KJ
Fat	10.14g
Saturated Fat	2.91g
Carbohydrate	11.50g
Fibre	1.60g

Spiced Lamb with Chillies

This is a fairly hot stir-fry dish, although you can, of course, make it less so by reducing the quantity of chillies.

INGREDIENTS

Serves 4

225g/8oz lean lamb fillet
120ml/4fl oz/½ cup natural (plain)
    low fat yogurt
1.5ml/¼ tsp ground cardamom
5ml/1 tsp crushed fresh root ginger
5ml/1 tsp crushed garlic
5ml/1 tsp chilli powder
5ml/1 tsp garam masala
5ml/1 tsp salt
15ml/1 tbsp oil
2 medium onions, chopped
1 bay leaf
300ml/½ pint/1¼ cups water
2 green chillies, sliced lengthways
2 red chillies, sliced lengthways
30ml/2 tbsp fresh coriander (cilantro)
    leaves

NUTRITIONAL NOTES	
Per Portion	
Energy	169Kcals/706KJ
Fat	8.13g
Saturated Fat	2.71g
Carbohydrate	10.01g
Fibre	1.32g

COOK'S TIP

Leaving the strips of lamb to marinate for an hour in the spicy yogurt mixture allows the flavour to penetrate right through the meat and also makes it beautifully tender, so it cooks quickly.

1 Using a sharp knife, remove any excess fat from the lamb and cut the meat into even-sized strips.

2 Mix together the yogurt, cardamom, crushed fresh root ginger, crushed garlic, chilli powder, garam masala and salt. Add the lamb and leave for about 1 hour to marinate.

3 Heat the oil in a wok or frying pan and fry the onions for 3-5 minutes until golden.

4 Add the bay leaf, then add the lamb with the yogurt and spice mixture and stir-fry for 2–3 minutes over medium heat.

5 Pour over the water, cover and cook for 15–20 minutes over a low heat, checking occasionally. Once the water has evaporated, stir-fry the mixture for 1 further minute.

6 Add the red and green chillies and the fresh coriander and serve hot.

Balti Lamb with Peas and Potatoes

Fresh mint leaves are used in this dish, but if they are unobtainable, use ready-minted frozen peas to bring an added freshness. Serve with plain rice.

Ingredients

Serves 4

225g/8oz lean spring lamb
120ml/4fl oz/½ cup natural (plain)
   low fat yogurt
1 cinnamon stick
2 green cardamom pods
3 black peppercorns
5ml/1 tsp crushed garlic
5ml/1 tsp crushed fresh root ginger
5ml/1 tsp chilli powder
5ml/1 tsp garam masala
5ml/1 tsp salt
30ml/2 tbsp roughly chopped
   fresh mint
15ml/1 tbsp oil
2 medium onions, sliced
300ml/½ pint/1¼ cups water
1 large potato, diced
115g/4oz/½ cup frozen peas
1 firm tomato, peeled, seeded
   and diced

1 Using a sharp knife, trim any excess fat from the lamb and cut the meat into strips. Place it in a bowl.

_____ Cook's Tip _____

This dish will improve in flavour if cooked in advance and kept in the refrigerator.

2 Add the yogurt, cinnamon, cardamoms, peppercorns, garlic, ginger, chilli powder, garam masala, salt and half the mint. Leave to marinate for about 2 hours.

3 Heat the oil in a wok or frying pan and fry the onions until golden brown. Stir in the lamb and the marinade and stir-fry for about 3 minutes.

Nutritional Notes	
Per Portion	
Energy	231Kcals/968KJ
Fat	8.47g
Saturated Fat	2.79g
Carbohydrate	22.72g
Fibre	3.73g

4 Pour in the water, lower the heat and cook until the meat is cooked right through, about 15 minutes, depending on the age of the lamb. Meanwhile, cook the potato in boiling water until just soft, but not mushy.

5 Add the peas and potato to the lamb and stir gently to mix.

6 Finally, add the remaining mint and the tomato and cook for a further 5 minutes before serving.

Spicy Spring Lamb Roast

There are a number of ways of
roasting lamb and several
different spice mixtures which
may be used to flavour the dish.
This is a popular variation.

INGREDIENTS

Serves 6
1.5kg/3–3½lb lean leg of spring lamb
5ml/1 tsp chilli powder
5ml/1 tsp crushed garlic
5ml/1 tsp ground coriander
5ml/1 tsp ground cumin
5ml/1 tsp salt
15ml/1 tbsp dried breadcrumbs
45ml/3 tbsp natural (plain)
   low fat yogurt
30ml/2 tbsp lemon juice
30ml/2 tbsp sultanas (golden raisins)
15ml/1 tbsp oil

For the garnish
mixed salad leaves
fresh coriander (cilantro)
2 tomatoes, quartered
1 large carrot, shredded
lemon wedges

NUTRITIONAL NOTES	
Per Portion	
Energy	265Kcals/1109KJ
Fat	13.40g
Saturated Fat	5.59g
Carbohydrate	8.90g
Fibre	0.70g

1 Preheat the oven to 180°C/350°F/
Gas 4. Trim any excess fat from
the lamb. Rinse and pat dry the joint
and set aside on a sheet of foil large
enough to enclose it completely.

2 In a medium bowl, mix together
the chilli powder, garlic, ground
coriander, ground cumin and salt.

3 Mix together in a food processor
the breadcrumbs, yogurt, lemon
juice and sultanas.

4 Add the contents of the food
processor to the spice mixture
together with the oil and mix together
well. Pour this on to the leg of lamb
and rub all over the meat.

5 Enclose the meat in the foil and
place in an ovenproof dish. Cook
in the oven for about 1½ hours.

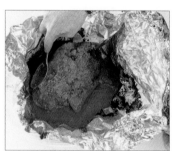

6 Remove the lamb from the oven,
open the foil and, using the back
of a spoon, spread the mixture evenly
over the meat. Return the lamb,
uncovered, to the oven for another
45 minutes or until it is cooked right
through and tender.

7 Slice the meat and serve with
the garnish ingredients.

—————— COOK'S TIP ——————

Make sure that the spice mixture is rubbed
all over the leg of lamb so that its flavour
penetrates all parts of the joint.

Stuffed Aubergines with Lamb

This is an attractive dish, using different coloured peppers in the lightly spiced stuffing mixture.

INGREDIENTS

Serves 4

2 medium aubergines (eggplants)
15ml/1 tbsp oil, plus extra for brushing
1 medium onion, sliced
5ml/1 tsp crushed fresh root ginger
5ml/1 tsp chilli powder
5ml/1 tsp crushed garlic
1.5ml/¼ tsp ground turmeric
5ml/1 tsp salt
5ml/1 tsp ground coriander
1 medium tomato, chopped
350g/12oz lean leg of lamb, minced (ground)
1 medium green (bell) pepper, seeded and roughly chopped
1 medium orange (bell) pepper, seeded and roughly chopped
30ml/2 tbsp chopped fresh coriander (cilantro)
plain rice, to serve

For the garnish

½ onion, sliced
2 cherry tomatoes, quartered
fresh coriander (cilantro)

1 Preheat the oven to 180°C/350°F/ Gas 4. Cut the aubergines in half lengthways and scoop out most of the flesh and discard. Place the aubergine shells cut side up in a lightly greased ovenproof dish.

2 In a medium pan, heat the oil and fry the sliced onions until golden brown in colour.

3 Gradually stir in the ginger, chilli powder, garlic, turmeric, salt and ground coriander. Add the chopped tomato, lower the heat and stir-fry for about 5 minutes.

4 Add the minced lamb and continue to stir-fry over medium heat for 7–10 minutes.

NUTRITIONAL NOTES	
Per Portion	
Energy	238Kcals/997KJ
Fat	11.70g
Saturated Fat	4.08g
Carbohydrate	12.60g
Fibre	5.90g

5 Add the chopped peppers and chopped fresh coriander to the lamb mixture and stir well.

6 Spoon the lamb mixture into the aubergine shells and brush the edge of the shells with a little oil. Bake in the oven for 1 hour or until cooked through and browned on top.

7 Serve with the garnish ingredients on a bed of plain rice.

VARIATION

For a special occasion, stuffed baby aubergines (eggplants) look particularly attractive. Use 4 small aubergines, leaving the stalks intact, and prepare and cook as described above, reducing the baking time slightly. Large tomatoes or courgettes (zucchini) make an excellent alternative to aubergines.

Balti Lamb in a Yogurt and Garam Masala Sauce

The lamb is first marinated then cooked slowly in a hot yogurt sauce and it is served with dried apricots which have been lightly sautéed in a low fat spread with cinnamon and cardamom.

INGREDIENTS

Serves 4

15ml/1 tbsp tomato purée (paste)
175ml/6fl oz/³/4 cup natural (plain) low fat yogurt
5ml/1 tsp garam masala
1.5ml/¼ tsp cumin seeds
5ml/1 tsp salt
5ml/1 tsp crushed garlic
5ml/1 tsp crushed fresh root ginger
5ml/1 tsp chilli powder
225g/8oz lean spring lamb, cut into strips
15ml/1 tbsp oil
2 medium onions, finely sliced
25g/1oz/2 tbsp low fat spread
2.5cm/1in cinnamon stick
2 green cardamom pods
5 apricots, ready-to-eat dried, quartered
15ml/1 tbsp fresh coriander (cilantro) leaves, to garnish

1 In a bowl blend together the tomato purée, yogurt, garam masala, cumin seeds, salt, garlic, ginger and chilli powder. Place the lamb in the sauce and leave to marinate in a cool place for about 1 hour.

2 Heat 10ml/2 tsp of the oil in a wok or frying pan and fry the onions over medium heat until they are crisp and golden brown.

3 Remove the onions using a slotted spoon, allow to cool and then grind down by processing briefly in a food processor or with a pestle and mortar. Reheat the oil remaining in the pan and return the onions to the wok.

NUTRITIONAL NOTES
Per Portion

Energy	221Kcals/922KJ
Fat	11.20g
Saturated Fat	3.64g
Carbohydrate	14.60g
Fibre	1.80g

——————— COOK'S TIP ———————

If you want this curry to be slightly hotter, increase the garam masala and chilli powder to 7.5ml/1½ tsp each.

4 Add the lamb and stir-fry for about 2 minutes. Cover with a lid, lower the heat and cook, stirring occasionally, for about 15 minutes or until the meat is cooked through. If required, add about 150ml/¼ pint/ ²/3 cup water during the cooking. Remove from the heat and set aside.

5 Heat the low fat spread with the remaining 5ml/1 tsp of oil and drop in the cinnamon stick and cardamoms. Add the dried apricots and stir over a low heat for about 2 minutes. Pour this over the lamb.

6 Serve garnished with the fresh coriander leaves.

Beef Madras

Madras curries originate from southern India and are aromatic, robust and pungent in flavour. This recipe uses stewing beef, but you can replace it with lean lamb if you prefer.

INGREDIENTS

Serves 4

900g/2lb lean stewing beef
15ml/1 tbsp oil
1 large onion, finely chopped
4 cloves
4 green cardamom pods
2 green chillies, finely chopped
2.5cm/1in piece root ginger, finely chopped
2 garlic cloves, crushed
2 dried red chillies
15ml/1 tbsp curry paste
10ml/2 tsp ground coriander
5ml/1 tsp ground cumin
2.5ml/½ tsp salt
150ml/¼ pint/⅔ cup beef stock
fresh coriander (cilantro), to garnish
Tomato Rice, to serve

1 Remove any visible fat from the beef and cut the meat into 2.5cm/1in cubes.

COOK'S TIP

When whole cardamom pods are used as a flavouring, they are not meant to be eaten. In India, they are left on the side of the plate, along with any bones.

2 Heat the oil in a large frying pan and stir-fry the onion, cloves and cardamom pods for about 5 minutes. Add the fresh green chillies, ginger, garlic and dried red chillies and fry for a further 2 minutes.

NUTRITIONAL NOTES	
Per Portion	
Energy	355Kcals/1487KJ
Fat	14.80g
Saturated Fat	4.66g
Carbohydrate	7.70g
Fibre	1.80g

3 Add the curry paste and fry for about 2 minutes. Add the beef and fry for 5–8 minutes until all the meat pieces are lightly browned.

4 Add the coriander, cumin, salt and stock. Cover and simmer gently for 1–1½ hours or until the meat is tender. Serve with Tomato Rice and garnish with fresh coriander.

Balti Beef

INGREDIENTS

Serves 4

1 red (bell) pepper
1 green (bell) pepper
15ml/1 tbsp oil
5ml/1 tsp cumin seeds
2.5ml/½ tsp fennel seeds
1 onion, cut into thick wedges
1 garlic clove, crushed
2.5cm/1in piece root ginger,
    finely chopped
1 red chilli, finely chopped
15ml/1 tbsp curry paste
2.5ml/½ tsp salt
675g/1½lb lean rump or fillet steak,
    cut into thick strips
naan bread, to serve

1 Cut the red and green peppers into 2.5cm/1in chunks.

2 Heat the oil in a non-stick wok or frying pan and fry the cumin and fennel seeds for about 2 minutes or until they begin to splutter. Add the onion, garlic, ginger and chilli and fry for a further 5 minutes.

3 Add the curry paste and salt and fry for a further 3–4 minutes.

4 Add the peppers and stir-fry for about 5 minutes. Stir in the beef strips and continue to fry for 10–12 minutes or until the meat is tender. Serve with warm naan bread.

NUTRITIONAL NOTES	
Per Portion	
Energy	278Kcals/1166KJ
Fat	11.60g
Saturated Fat	3.52g
Carbohydrate	7.70g
Fibre	2.50g

Beef Vindaloo

A fiery dish originally from Goa, a "vindaloo" curry is made using a unique blend of hot aromatic spices and vinegar to give it a distinctive flavour.

INGREDIENTS

Serves 6

15ml/1 tbsp cumin seeds
4 dried red chillies
5ml/1 tsp black peppercorns
5 green cardamom pods, seeds only
5ml/1 tsp fenugreek seeds
5ml/1 tsp black mustard seeds
2.5ml/½ tsp salt
2.5ml/½ tsp demerara (raw) sugar
60ml/4 tbsp white wine vinegar
30ml/2 tbsp oil
1 large onion, finely chopped
900g/2lb lean stewing beef, cut
  into 2.5cm/1in cubes
2.5cm/1in piece root ginger,
  finely chopped
1 garlic clove, crushed
10ml/2 tsp ground coriander
2.5ml/½ tsp ground turmeric
plain and yellow rice, to serve

NUTRITIONAL NOTES	
Per Portion	
Energy	269Kcals/1127KJ
Fat	11.60g
Saturated Fat	3.28g
Carbohydrate	7.30g
Fibre	0.60g

COOK'S TIP

To make plain and yellow rice, infuse a pinch of saffron strands or dissolve a little ground turmeric in 15ml/1 tbsp hot water. Stir into half the cooked rice until uniformly yellow. Carefully mix the yellow rice into the plain rice.

1 Put the cumin seeds, chillies, peppercorns, cardamom seeds, fenugreek seeds and mustard seeds into a coffee grinder (or a mortar and pestle) and grind to a fine powder. Add the salt, sugar and white wine vinegar and mix to a thin paste.

2 Heat 15ml/1 tbsp of the oil in a large frying pan and fry the onion for 10 minutes. Put the onions and the spice mixture into a food processor or blender and process to a coarse paste.

3 Heat the remaining oil in the frying pan and fry the meat cubes for about 10 minutes until lightly browned. Remove the beef cubes with a slotted spoon and set aside.

4 Add the ginger and garlic and fry for 2 minutes. Stir in the ground coriander and turmeric and fry for a further 2 minutes.

5 Add the spice and onion paste and fry for about 5 minutes.

6 Return the beef cubes to the pan together with 300ml/½ pint/ 1¼ cups water. Cover and simmer for 1–1½ hours or until the meat is tender. Serve with plain and yellow rice.

Beef with Green Beans

Green beans cooked with beef is a variation on the traditional recipe using lamb. The red (bell) pepper used here makes this dish colourful as well as delicious.

Ingredients

Serves 4
275g/10oz fine green beans, cut into 2.5cm/1in pieces
15ml/1 tbsp oil
1 medium onion, sliced
5ml/1 tsp crushed fresh root ginger
5ml/1 tsp crushed garlic
5ml/1 tsp chilli powder
6.5ml/1¼ tsp salt
1.5ml/¼ tsp turmeric
2 tomatoes, chopped
450g/1lb lean beef, cubed
1.2 litres/2 pints/5 cups water
1 red (bell) pepper, seeded and sliced
15ml/1 tbsp chopped fresh coriander (cilantro)
2 green chillies, chopped
warm chappatis, to serve (optional)

Nutritional Notes	
Per Portion	
Energy	242Kcals/1012KJ
Fat	11.60g
Saturated Fat	2.91g
Carbohydrate	9.30g
Fibre	3.00g

_____ Cook's Tip _____

If you blanch the green beans in boiling water, drain well and then rinse them quickly under cold running water and drain again, it helps to preserve their bright green colour. This can be done quite a bit ahead of the final cooking time.

1 Blanch the beans in boiling water for 3–4 minutes, then rinse under cold running water, drain and set aside.

2 Heat the oil in a large pan and gently fry the onion until golden brown in colour.

3 Mix together the crushed fresh root ginger, crushed garlic, chilli powder, salt, turmeric and chopped tomatoes. Spoon this mixture into the onion and stir-fry for 5–7 minutes.

4 Add the beef and stir-fry for a further 3 minutes. Pour in the water, bring to the boil and lower the heat. Cover the pan and cook for 45–60 minutes until most of the water has evaporated and the meat is tender.

5 Add the green beans and mix everything together well.

6 Finally, add the red pepper, fresh coriander and green chillies and cook, stirring, for a further 7–10 minutes, making sure the beans are tender before serving.

7 Serve the beef hot, accompanied by warm chappatis (optional).

CHICKEN DISHES

Chicken is an obvious choice for a healthy diet as it is low in fat and much of the fat it contains is low in saturates, and if you cut off all the skin before cooking, you will reduce the fat content of the dish even further. Chicken is also a very versatile meat, adapting well to different cooking methods and going well with a variety of ingredients, as recipes in this section, ranging from hot Balti Chicken Vindaloo to mild Chicken Korma, show.

Chicken Tikka Masala

Tender chicken pieces are cooked in a creamy, spicy tomato sauce and served on naan bread.

INGREDIENTS

Serves 4

675g/1½lb chicken breast fillets, skinned
90ml/6 tbsp tikka paste
120ml/4fl oz/½ cup natural (plain) low fat yogurt
15ml/1 tbsp oil
1 onion, chopped
1 garlic clove, crushed
1 green chilli, seeded and chopped
2.5cm/1in piece root ginger, grated
15ml/1 tbsp tomato purée (paste)
250ml/8fl oz/1 cup water
a little melted butter
15ml/1 tbsp lemon juice
fresh coriander (cilantro) sprigs, natural (plain) low fat yogurt and toasted cumin seeds, to garnish
naan bread, to serve

NUTRITIONAL NOTES	
Per Portion	
Energy	315Kcals/1321KJ
Fat	12.50g
Saturated Fat	4.00g
Carbohydrate	7.50g
Fibre	0.60g

--- COOK'S TIP ---

Soak the wooden skewers in cold water before using to prevent them from burning while under the grill (broiler).

1 Remove any visible fat from the chicken and cut the meat into 2.5cm/1in cubes. Put 45ml/3 tbsp of the tikka paste and 60ml/4 tbsp of the yogurt into a bowl. Add the chicken and leave to marinate for 20 minutes.

2 For the tikka sauce, heat the oil in a pan and fry the onion, garlic, chilli and ginger for 5 minutes. Add the remaining tikka paste and fry for 2 minutes. Add the tomato purée and water, bring to the boil and simmer for 15 minutes.

3 Meanwhile, thread the chicken pieces on to wooden kebab skewers. Preheat the grill (broiler).

4 Brush the chicken pieces lightly with melted butter and grill (broil) under medium heat for 15 minutes, turning the skewers occasionally.

5 Put the tikka sauce into a food processor or blender and process until smooth. Return to the pan.

6 Add the remaining yogurt and lemon juice, remove the grilled chicken pieces from the skewers and add to the pan, then simmer for 5 minutes. Garnish with fresh coriander, yogurt and toasted cumin seeds and serve on naan bread.

Tandoori Chicken

A most popular Indian/Pakistani chicken dish which is cooked in a clay oven called a *tandoor*, this is extremely popular in the West and appears on the majority of restaurant menus. Although the authentic tandoori flavour is very difficult to achieve in conventional ovens, this version still makes a very tasty dish.

INGREDIENTS

Serves 4

4 chicken quarters, skinned
175ml/6fl oz/¾ cup natural (plain) low fat yogurt
5ml/1 tsp garam masala
5ml/1 tsp crushed fresh root ginger
5ml/1 tsp crushed garlic
7.5ml/1½ tsp chilli powder
1.5ml/¼ tsp ground turmeric
5ml/1 tsp ground coriander
15ml/1 tbsp lemon juice
5ml/1 tsp salt
few drops of red food colouring
15ml/1 tbsp oil
mixed salad leaves and lime wedges, to garnish

1 Rinse and pat dry the chicken quarters. Make two deep slits in the flesh of each piece, place in a dish and set aside.

_____ COOK'S TIP _____

The traditional bright red colour is derived from food colouring. This is only optional and may be omitted if you wish.

2 Mix together the yogurt, garam masala, ginger, garlic, chilli powder, turmeric, coriander, lemon juice, salt, red food colouring and oil, and beat so that all the ingredients are well combined.

NUTRITIONAL NOTES	
Per Portion	
Energy	300Kcals/1256KJ
Fat	12.00g
Saturated Fat	3.39g
Carbohydrate	5.90g
Fibre	0.20g

3 Cover the chicken quarters with the spice mixture and leave to marinate for about 3 hours.

4 Preheat the oven to 240°C/475°F/ Gas 9. Transfer the chicken pieces to an ovenproof dish.

5 Bake the chicken in the oven for 20–25 minutes or until the chicken is cooked right through and evenly browned on top.

6 Remove from the oven, transfer to a serving dish and garnish with the salad leaves and lime wedges.

Chicken Jalfrezi

A Jalfrezi curry is a stir-fried dish cooked with onions, ginger and garlic in a rich pepper sauce.

INGREDIENTS

Serves 4

675g/1½lb chicken breast fillets, skinned
15ml/1 tbsp oil
5ml/1 tsp cumin seeds
1 onion, finely chopped
1 green (bell) pepper, seeded and
   finely chopped
1 red (bell) pepper, seeded and
   finely chopped
1 garlic clove, crushed
2cm/¾in piece root ginger,
   finely chopped
15ml/1 tbsp curry paste
1.5ml/¼ tsp chilli powder
5ml/1 tsp ground coriander
5ml/1 tsp ground cumin
2.5ml/½ tsp salt
400g/14oz can chopped tomatoes
30ml/2 tbsp chopped fresh coriander
   (cilantro), plus extra to garnish
plain rice, to serve

1 Remove any visible fat from the chicken and cut the meat into 2.5cm/1in cubes.

NUTRITIONAL NOTES	
Per Portion	
Energy	291Kcals/1224KJ
Fat	9.80g
Saturated Fat	2.24g
Carbohydrate	11.70g
Fibre	3.50g

2 Heat the oil in a wok or frying pan and fry the cumin seeds for 2 minutes until they splutter. Add the onion, peppers, garlic and ginger and fry for 6–8 minutes.

3 Add the curry paste and fry for about 2 minutes. Stir in the chilli powder, ground coriander, cumin and salt and add 15ml/1 tbsp water; fry for a further 2 minutes.

4 Add the chicken cubes and fry for about 5 minutes. Add the canned tomatoes and chopped fresh coriander. Cover the wok or frying pan with a lid and cook for about 15 minutes or until the chicken cubes are tender. Garnish with a sprig of fresh coriander and serve with rice.

Balti Chicken Vindaloo

This is considered rather a hot curry and is probably one of the best-known Indian dishes, especially in the West.

INGREDIENTS

Serves 4

1 large potato
150ml/¼ pint/⅔ cup malt vinegar
7.5ml/1½ tsp crushed coriander seeds
5ml/1 tsp crushed cumin seeds
7.5ml/1½ tsp chilli powder
1.5ml/¼ tsp ground turmeric
5ml/1 tsp crushed garlic
5ml/1 tsp crushed fresh root ginger
5ml/1 tsp salt
7.5ml/1½ tsp paprika
15ml/1 tbsp tomato purée (paste)
large pinch of ground fenugreek
300ml/½ pint/1¼ cups water
225g/8oz chicken breast fillets, skinned
   and cubed
15ml/1 tbsp oil
2 medium onions, sliced
4 curry leaves
2 green chillies, chopped

1 Peel the potato, cut it into large, irregular shapes, place in a bowl of water and set aside.

_____ COOK'S TIP _____

The best thing to drink with a hot curry is either iced water or a yogurt-based lassi.

2 Mix together the vinegar, coriander, cumin, chilli powder, turmeric, garlic, ginger, salt, paprika, tomato purée, fenugreek and water.

3 Pour this spice mixture over the chicken and set aside.

4 Heat the oil in a wok or frying pan and quickly fry the onions with the curry leaves for 3–4 minutes without burning.

5 Lower the heat and add the chicken mixture to the pan with the spices. Continue to stir-fry for a further 2 minutes. Drain the potato pieces and add to the pan. Cover with a lid and cook over a medium to low heat for 5–7 minutes or until the sauce has thickened slightly and the chicken and potatoes are cooked through.

6 Add the chopped green chillies before serving.

NUTRITIONAL NOTES	
Per Portion	
Energy	168Kcals/704KJ
Fat	4.20g
Saturated Fat	0.60g
Carbohydrate	17.65g
Fibre	2.04g

Chicken Korma

Although kormas are traditionally rich and high in fat, this recipe uses low fat yogurt instead of cream, which keeps down the fat content. To prevent the yogurt from curdling, add it very slowly to the sauce and keep stirring until it is incorporated.

INGREDIENTS

Serves 4

675g/1½lb chicken breast fillets, skinned
2 garlic cloves, crushed
2.5cm/1in piece root ginger, chopped
15ml/1 tbsp oil
3 green cardamom pods
1 onion, finely chopped
10ml/2 tsp ground cumin
1.5ml/¼ tsp salt
300ml/½ pint/1¼ cups natural (plain) low fat yogurt
toasted flaked (sliced) almonds (optional) and a fresh coriander (cilantro) sprig, to garnish
plain rice, to serve

1 Remove any visible fat from the chicken breasts and cut the meat into 2.5cm/1in cubes.

_____ COOK'S TIP _____

Traditionally, kormas are spicy dishes with a rich, creamy texture. They are not meant to be very hot curries.

2 Put the garlic and ginger into a food processor or blender with 30ml/2 tbsp water and process to a smooth, creamy paste.

3 Heat the oil in a large pan and cook the chicken cubes for 8–10 minutes until browned on all sides. Remove the chicken cubes with a slotted spoon and set aside.

4 Add the cardamom pods and fry for 2 minutes. Add the onion and fry for a further 5 minutes.

NUTRITIONAL NOTES	
Per Portion	
Energy	288Kcals/1211KJ
Fat	9.30g
Saturated Fat	2.54g
Carbohydrate	9.80g
Fibre	0.50g

5 Stir in the garlic and ginger paste, cumin and salt and cook, stirring, for a further 5 minutes.

6 Add half the yogurt, stirring in a tablespoonful at a time, and cook over a low heat, until it has all been absorbed. Return the chicken to the pan. Cover and simmer over a low heat for 5–6 minutes or until the chicken is tender. Add the remaining yogurt and simmer for a further 5 minutes. Garnish with toasted flaked almonds and coriander and serve with rice.

Chicken Dhansak

Dhansak curries originate from
the Parsee community and are
traditionally made with a mixture
of lentils and meat.

Ingredients

Serves 4

75g/3oz/½ cup green lentils
475ml/16fl oz/2 cups chicken stock
15ml/1 tbsp oil
5ml/1 tsp cumin seeds
2 curry leaves
1 onion, finely chopped
2.5cm/1in piece root ginger, chopped
1 green chilli, finely chopped
5ml/1 tsp ground cumin
5ml/1 tsp ground coriander
1.5ml/¼ tsp salt
1.5ml/¼ tsp chilli powder
400g/14oz can chopped tomatoes
8 chicken pieces, skinned
60ml/4 tbsp chopped fresh coriander
   (cilantro), plus extra to garnish
5ml/1 tsp garam masala
plain and yellow rice, to serve

1 Rinse the lentils under cold
running water. Put into a pan with
the stock. Bring to the boil, cover and
simmer for about 15–20 minutes. Put
the lentils and stock to one side.

2 Heat the oil in a large pan and fry
the cumin seeds and curry leaves
for 2 minutes. Add the onion, ginger
and chilli and fry for about 5 minutes.
Stir in the cumin, coriander, salt and
chilli powder with 30ml/2 tbsp water.

Nutritional Notes	
Per Portion	
Energy	328Kcals/1376KJ
Fat	10.80g
Saturated Fat	2.54g
Carbohydrate	19.70g
Fibre	3.50g

3 Add the tomatoes and the chicken
pieces to the spices. Cover and
cook for 10–15 minutes.

4 Add the lentils and stock, chopped
fresh coriander and garam masala
and cook for a further 10 minutes or
until the chicken is tender. Garnish
with fresh coriander and serve with
spiced plain and yellow rice.

Hot Chilli Chicken

Not for the faint-hearted, this fiery, hot curry is made with a spicy chilli masala paste.

INGREDIENTS

Serves 4

30ml/2 tbsp tomato purée (paste)
2 garlic cloves, roughly chopped
2 fresh green chillies, roughly chopped
5 dried red chillies
2.5ml/½ tsp salt
1.5ml/¼ tsp sugar
5ml/1 tsp chilli powder
2.5ml/½ tsp paprika
15ml/1 tbsp curry paste
15ml/1 tbsp oil
2.5ml/½ tsp cumin seeds
1 onion, finely chopped
2 bay leaves
5ml/1 tsp ground coriander
5ml/1 tsp ground cumin
1.5ml/¼ tsp ground turmeric
400g/14oz can chopped tomatoes
150ml/¼ pint/⅔ cup water
8 chicken thigh fillets, skinned
5ml/1 tsp garam masala
sliced green chillies, to garnish
chappatis and natural (plain) low fat
    yogurt, to serve

1 Put the tomato purée, chopped garlic cloves, fresh green chillies and the dried red chillies into a food processor or blender. Add the salt, sugar, chilli powder, paprika and curry paste and process all the ingredients to a smooth paste.

2 Heat the oil in a large pan and fry the cumin seeds for 2 minutes. Add the onion and bay leaves and fry for about 5 minutes.

3 Add the chilli paste and fry for 2–3 minutes. Add the coriander, cumin and turmeric and cook for 2 minutes. Add the tomatoes and water. Bring to the boil and simmer for 5 minutes until the sauce thickens.

4 Add the chicken and garam masala. Cover and simmer for 25–30 minutes until the chicken is tender. Garnish with sliced green chillies and serve with chappatis and natural low fat yogurt.

NUTRITIONAL NOTES	
Per Portion	
Energy	290Kcals/1212KJ
Fat	13.00g
Saturated Fat	3.50g
Carbohydrate	11.60g
Fibre	1.40g

Balti Chicken Madras

This is a fairly hot chicken curry which is good served with either plain boiled rice, pilau rice or naan bread.

INGREDIENTS

Serves 4

275g/10oz chicken breast fillets, skinned
45ml/3 tbsp tomato purée (paste)
large pinch of ground fenugreek
1.5ml/¼ tsp ground fennel seeds
5ml/1 tsp crushed fresh root ginger
7.5ml/1½ tsp ground coriander
5ml/1 tsp crushed garlic
5ml/1 tsp chilli powder
1.5ml/¼ tsp ground turmeric
30ml/2 tbsp lemon juice
5ml/1 tsp salt
300ml/½ pint/1¼ cups water
15ml/1 tbsp oil
2 medium onions, diced
2–4 curry leaves
2 green chillies, seeded and chopped
15ml/1 tbsp fresh coriander (cilantro)
  leaves

NUTRITIONAL NOTES	
Per Portion	
Energy	141Kcals/591KJ
Fat	4.11g
Saturated Fat	0.60g
Carbohydrate	8.60g
Fibre	1.53g

--------- COOK'S TIP ---------

Always take care not to be over-generous when you are using ground fenugreek as it can be quite bitter.

1 Remove any visible fat from the chicken breasts and cut the meat into bitesize cubes.

2 Mix the tomato purée in a bowl with the fenugreek, fennel seeds, ginger, coriander, garlic, chilli powder, turmeric, lemon juice, salt and water.

3 Heat the oil in a wok or frying pan and fry the onions together with the curry leaves until the onions are golden brown.

4 Add the chicken pieces to the onions and stir for about 1 minute to seal the meat.

5 Next, pour in the prepared spice mixture and continue to stir the chicken for about 2 minutes.

6 Lower the heat and cook for 8–10 minutes. Add the chillies and fresh coriander and serve at once.

Chicken Saag

A mildly spiced dish using a popular combination of spinach and chicken. This recipe is best made using fresh spinach, but if this is unavailable you can use frozen instead.

INGREDIENTS

Serves 4

225g/8oz fresh spinach leaves, washed but not dried
2.5cm/1in piece root ginger, grated
2 garlic cloves, crushed
1 green chilli, roughly chopped
200ml/7fl oz/scant 1 cup water
15ml/1 tbsp oil
2 bay leaves
1.5ml/¼ tsp black peppercorns
1 onion, finely chopped
4 tomatoes, skinned and finely chopped
10ml/2 tsp curry powder
5ml/1 tsp salt
5ml/1 tsp chilli powder
45ml/3 tbsp natural (plain) low fat yogurt
8 chicken thigh fillets, skinned
natural (plain) low fat yogurt and chilli powder, to garnish
naan bread, to serve

1 Cook the spinach leaves, without water, in a tightly covered pan for 5 minutes. Put the cooked spinach, ginger, garlic and chilli with 50ml/2fl oz/¼ cup of the water into a food processor or blender and process to a thick purée. Set aside.

2 Heat the oil in a large pan, add the bay leaves and black peppercorns and fry for 2 minutes. Add the onion and fry for a further 6–8 minutes or until the onion has browned.

3 Add the tomatoes and simmer for about 5 minutes. Stir in the curry powder, salt and chilli powder and cook for 2 minutes.

NUTRITIONAL NOTES	
Per Portion	
Energy	283Kcals/1182KJ
Fat	12.70g
Saturated Fat	3.48g
Carbohydrate	9.70g
Fibre	3.10g

4 Add the spinach purée and 150ml/¼ pint/⅔ cup water; simmer for 5 minutes.

5 Add the yogurt, 15ml/1 tbsp at a time, and simmer for 5 minutes.

6 Add the chicken thighs. Cover and cook for 25–30 minutes until the chicken is tender. Serve on naan bread, drizzle over some yogurt and dust with chilli powder.

Jeera Chicken

An aromatic dish with a delicious, distinctive taste of cumin. Serve simply with cooling Cucumber Raita.

INGREDIENTS

Serves 4

45ml/3 tbsp cumin seeds
15ml/1 tbsp oil
2.5ml/½ tsp black peppercorns
4 green cardamom pods
2 green chillies, finely chopped
2 garlic cloves, crushed
2.5cm/1in piece root ginger, grated
5ml/1 tsp ground coriander
10ml/2 tsp ground cumin
2.5ml/½ tsp salt
8 chicken portions, such as thighs and
    drumsticks, skinned
5ml/1 tsp garam masala
fresh coriander (cilantro) and chilli
    powder, to garnish
Cucumber Raita, to serve

1 Dry-roast 15ml/1 tbsp of the cumin seeds for 5 minutes and then set aside.

_____ COOK'S TIP _____

Dry-roast the cumin seeds in a small, heavy frying pan over medium heat, stirring them until they turn a few shades darker and give off a wonderful roasted aroma.

2 Heat the oil in a large heavy pan and fry the remaining cumin seeds, black peppercorns and cardamoms for about 2–3 minutes.

3 Add the chillies, garlic and ginger and fry for about 2 minutes.

4 Add the ground coriander, ground cumin and salt and cook for a further 2–3 minutes.

5 Add the chicken. Cover and simmer for 20–25 minutes.

6 Add the garam masala and reserved toasted cumin seeds and cook for a further 5 minutes. Garnish with fresh coriander and chilli powder and serve with Cucumber Raita.

NUTRITIONAL NOTES	
Per Portion	
Energy	286Kcals/1198KJ
Fat	14.10g
Saturated Fat	3.19g
Carbohydrate	7.60g
Fibre	0.10g

Balti Chicken Curry

Tender pieces of chicken are lightly cooked with fresh vegetables and aromatic spices in the traditional Balti style.

INGREDIENTS

Serves 4

675g/1½lb chicken breast fillets, skinned
15ml/1 tbsp oil
2.5ml/½ tsp cumin seeds
2.5ml/½ tsp fennel seeds
1 onion, thickly sliced
2 garlic cloves, crushed
2.5cm/1in piece root ginger, chopped
15ml/1 tbsp curry paste
225g/8oz broccoli, broken into florets
4 tomatoes, cut into thick wedges
5ml/1 tsp garam masala
30ml/2 tbsp chopped fresh coriander (cilantro)
naan bread, to serve

1 Remove any visible fat from the chicken and cut the meat into 2.5cm/1in cubes.

NUTRITIONAL NOTES *Per Portion*	
Energy	286Kcals/1201KJ
Fat	9.80g
Saturated Fat	2.19g
Carbohydrate	8.50g
Fibre	3.70g

2 Heat the oil in a wok or frying pan and fry the cumin and fennel seeds for 2 minutes until the seeds begin to splutter. Add the onion, garlic and ginger and cook for 5–7 minutes. Stir in the curry paste and cook for a further 2–3 minutes.

3 Add the broccoli florets and fry for about 5 minutes. Add the chicken cubes and fry for 5–8 minutes.

4 Add the tomato wedges to the wok with the garam masala and the chopped fresh coriander. Cook the curry for a further 5–10 minutes or until the chicken cubes are tender. Serve with naan bread.

Chicken Dopiazza

Dopiazza translates literally as "two onions" and describes this chicken dish in which two types of onion – large and small – are used at different stages during the cooking process.

INGREDIENTS

Serves 4

30ml/2 tbsp oil
8 small onions, halved
2 bay leaves
8 green cardamom pods
4 cloves
3 dried red chillies
8 black peppercorns
2 onions, finely chopped
2 garlic cloves, crushed
2.5cm/1in piece root ginger,
  finely chopped
5ml/1 tsp ground coriander
5ml/1 tsp ground cumin
2.5ml/½ tsp ground turmeric
5ml/1 tsp chilli powder
2.5ml/½ tsp salt
4 tomatoes, skinned and finely chopped
120ml/4fl oz/½ cup water
8 chicken portions, such as thighs and
  drumsticks, skinned
plain rice, to serve

--- COOK'S TIP ---

Soak the small onions in boiling water for 2–3 minutes to make them easier to peel.

NUTRITIONAL NOTES	
Per Portion	
Energy	352Kcals/1469KJ
Fat	15.10g
Saturated Fat	3.67g
Carbohydrate	22.60g
Fibre	3.90g

1 Heat half the oil in a large heavy pan and fry the small onions for 10 minutes, or until golden brown. Remove and set aside.

3 Add the tomatoes and water and simmer for 5 minutes until the sauce thickens. Add the chicken and cook for about 15 minutes.

2 Add the remaining oil and fry the bay leaves, cardamoms, cloves, chillies and peppercorns for 2 minutes. Add the onions, garlic and ginger and fry for 5 minutes. Stir in the ground spices and salt and cook for 2 minutes.

4 Add the reserved small onions, then cover and cook for a further 10 minutes, or until the chicken is tender. Serve with plain boiled rice.

Balti Chicken in Hara Masala Sauce

This chicken dish can be served as an accompaniment to any of the rice dishes in this book.

INGREDIENTS

Serves 4

1 crisp green eating apple, peeled, cored and cut into small cubes
60ml/4 tbsp fresh coriander (cilantro) leaves
30ml/2 tbsp fresh mint leaves
120ml/4fl oz/½ cup natural (plain) low fat yogurt
45ml/3 tbsp low fat fromage frais or crème fraîche
2 medium green chillies, seeded and chopped
1 bunch spring onions (scallions), chopped
5ml/1 tsp salt
5ml/1 tsp sugar
5ml/1 tsp crushed garlic
5ml/1 tsp crushed fresh root ginger
15ml/1 tbsp oil
225g/8oz chicken breast fillets, skinned and cubed
25g/1oz/⅙ cup sultanas (golden raisins)

1 Place the apple, 45ml/3 tbsp of the coriander, the mint, yogurt, fromage frais or crème fraîche, chillies, spring onions, salt, sugar, garlic and ginger in a food processor and process for about 1 minute, using the pulsing action.

2 Heat the oil in a wok or heavy frying pan, pour in the yogurt mixture and cook over a low heat for about 2 minutes.

NUTRITIONAL NOTES	
Per Portion	
Energy	158Kcals/666KJ
Fat	4.37g
Saturated Fat	1.69g
Carbohydrate	14.54g
Fibre	1.08g

3 Next, add the chicken fillets and blend everything together. Cook over medium/low heat for 12–15 minutes or until the chicken is fully cooked through.

4 Finally, add the sultanas and remaining 15ml/1 tbsp fresh coriander leaves before serving.

--- COOK'S TIP ---

This dish makes an attractive centrepiece for a dinner-party.

Balti Chicken in a Thick Creamy Coconut Sauce

If you like the flavour of coconut, you will really love this aromatic curry.

INGREDIENTS

Serves 4

15ml/1 tbsp ground almonds
15ml/1 tbsp desiccated (dry unsweetened shredded) coconut
75ml/3fl oz/¹/₃ cup coconut milk
175g/6oz/²/₃ cup low fat fromage frais or crème fraîche
7.5ml/1½ tsp ground coriander
5ml/1 tsp chilli powder
5ml/1 tsp crushed garlic
7.5ml/1½ tsp crushed fresh root ginger
5ml/1 tsp salt
15ml/1 tbsp oil
225g/8oz boneless chicken fillets, skinned and cubed
3 green cardamom pods
1 bay leaf
1 dried red chilli, crushed
30ml/2 tbsp chopped fresh coriander (cilantro)

1 Using a heavy pan, dry-roast the ground almonds and desiccated coconut until they turn just a shade darker. Transfer the nut mixture to a mixing bowl.

NUTRITIONAL NOTES	
Per Portion	
Energy	166Kcals/696KJ
Fat	8.30g
Saturated Fat	2.84g
Carbohydrate	6.38g
Fibre	0.95g

2 Add the coconut milk, fromage frais or crème fraîche, ground coriander, chilli powder, garlic, ginger and salt to the mixing bowl.

3 Heat the oil in a wok or heavy frying pan and add the chicken cubes, cardamoms and bay leaf. Stir-fry for about 2 minutes to seal the chicken but not cook it.

4 Pour in the coconut milk mixture and blend everything together. Lower the heat, add the chilli and fresh coriander, cover and cook for 10–12 minutes, stirring occasionally. Uncover, then stir and cook for a further 2 minutes before serving, making sure the chicken is cooked.

Chicken in a Cashew Nut Sauce

This strongly flavoured chicken dish has a deliciously thick and nutty sauce, and is best served with plain boiled rice.

INGREDIENTS

Serves 4
2 medium onions
30ml/2 tbsp tomato purée (paste)
50g/2oz/⅓ cup cashew nuts
7.5ml/1½ tsp garam masala
5ml/1 tsp crushed garlic
5ml/1 tsp chilli powder
15ml/1 tbsp lemon juice
1.5ml/¼ tsp ground turmeric
5ml/1 tsp salt
15ml/1 tbsp natural (plain) low fat yogurt
30ml/2 tbsp oil
30ml/2 tbsp chopped fresh coriander (cilantro)
15ml/1 tbsp sultanas (golden raisins)
450g/1lb boneless chicken fillets, skinned and cubed
175g/6oz/2½ cups button (white) mushrooms
300ml/½ pint/1¼ cups water

1 Cut the onions into quarters, place in a food processor or blender and process for about 1 minute.

2 Add the tomato purée, cashew nuts, garam masala, garlic, chilli powder, lemon juice, turmeric, salt and yogurt to the processed onions.

3 Process all the spice ingredients in the food processor for a further 1–1½ minutes.

4 In a pan, heat the oil, lower the heat to medium and pour in the spice mixture from the food processor. Fry for 2 minutes, lowering the heat if necessary.

5 When the spice mixture is lightly cooked, add half the chopped fresh coriander, the sultanas and the chicken cubes and continue to stir-fry for a further 1 minute.

_____ COOK'S TIP _____

Cut the chicken into small, equal-sized cubes for quick and even cooking.

6 Add the mushrooms, pour in the water and bring to a simmer. Cover the pan and cook over a low heat for about 10 minutes.

7 After this time, check that the chicken is cooked through and the sauce is thick. Cook for a little longer if necessary and serve garnished with the remaining fresh coriander.

NUTRITIONAL NOTES	
Per Portion	
Energy	286Kcals/1199KJ
Fat	13.30g
Saturated Fat	2.39g
Carbohydrate	12.90g
Fibre	2.10g

Chicken with Green Mango

Green, unripe mango is used for making various dishes on the Indian sub-continent, including pickles, chutneys and some meat, chicken and vegetable dishes. This is a fairly simple chicken dish to prepare and is good served with rice and dhal.

INGREDIENTS

Serves 4

1 medium green mango
450g/1lb chicken breast fillets, skinned
   and cubed
1.5ml/¼ tsp onion seeds
5ml/1 tsp crushed fresh root ginger
2.5ml/½ tsp crushed garlic
5ml/1 tsp chilli powder
1.5ml/¼ tsp ground turmeric
5ml/1 tsp salt
5ml/1 tsp ground coriander
30ml/2 tbsp oil
2 medium onions, sliced
4 curry leaves
300ml/½ pint/1¼ cups water
2 medium tomatoes, quartered
2 green chillies, chopped
30ml/2 tbsp chopped fresh coriander
   (cilantro)

1 To prepare the mango, peel the skin and slice the flesh thickly. Discard the stone (pit) from the middle. Place the mango slices in a small bowl, cover and set aside.

2 Place the chicken cubes in a bowl and add the onion seeds, ginger, garlic, chilli powder, turmeric, salt and ground coriander. Mix the spices into the chicken and add half the mango slices to this mixture as well.

3 In a medium heavy pan, heat the oil and fry the sliced onions until golden brown in colour. Add the curry leaves.

4 Gradually add the chicken, stirring all the time.

5 Pour in the water, lower the heat and cook for about 12–15 minutes, stirring occasionally, until the chicken is cooked through and the water has been absorbed.

6 Add the remaining mango slices, the tomatoes, green chillies and fresh coriander and serve hot.

VARIATION

A good, firm cooking apple can be used instead of unripe green mango, if wished. Prepare and cook in exactly the same way.

NUTRITIONAL NOTES
Per Portion

Energy	281Kcals/1172KJ
Fat	11.20g
Saturated Fat	2.44g
Carbohydrate	20.60g
Fibre	3.60g

Spicy Masala Chicken

These grilled (broiled) chicken pieces have a sweet-and-sour taste. They can either be served cold with a salad and rice or hot with Masala Mashed Potatoes.

INGREDIENTS

Serves 6

12 chicken thigh fillets, skinned
90ml/6 tbsp lemon juice
5ml/1 tsp crushed fresh root ginger
5ml/1 tsp crushed garlic
5ml/1 tsp crushed dried red chillies
5ml/1 tsp salt
5ml/1 tsp soft brown sugar
30ml/2 tbsp clear honey
30ml/2 tbsp chopped fresh coriander (cilantro), plus extra to garnish
1 green chilli, finely chopped
30ml/2 tbsp vegetable oil
yellow rice and salad, to serve

1 Prick the chicken thighs with a fork, rinse them, pat dry with absorbent paper and set aside in a bowl.

2 In a large mixing bowl, mix together the lemon juice, ginger, garlic, crushed dried red chillies, salt, sugar and honey.

3 Transfer the chicken thighs to the spice mixture and coat well. Set aside for about 45 minutes.

4 Preheat the grill (broiler) to medium. Add the coriander and chopped green chilli to the chicken thighs and place them in an oven dish.

5 Pour any remaining marinade over the chicken and brush with the oil.

6 Grill (broil) the chicken thighs for 15–20 minutes, turning and basting with the marinade occasionally, until cooked through and browned.

7 Serve cold, garnished with fresh coriander and accompanied by yellow rice and salad.

NUTRITIONAL NOTES	
Per Portion	
Energy	243Kcals/1017KJ
Fat	12.00g
Saturated Fat	3.18g
Carbohydrate	5.30g
Fibre	0.00g

_____ COOK'S TIP _____

Substitute small, lean lamb chops for the chicken thighs as a tasty alternative.

Balti Chicken in Orange and Black Pepper Sauce

Use virtually fat-free fromage frais to give this sauce a rich creamy flavour without the fat.

INGREDIENTS

Serves 4

225g/8oz low fat fromage frais or
  crème fraîche
50ml/2fl oz/¼ cup natural (plain)
  low fat yogurt
120ml/4fl oz/½ cup orange juice
7.5ml/1½ tsp crushed fresh root ginger
5ml/1 tsp crushed garlic
5ml/1 tsp ground black pepper
5ml/1 tsp salt
5ml/1 tsp ground coriander
1 small chicken, about 675g/1½lb,
  skinned and cut into 8 pieces
15ml/1 tbsp oil
1 bay leaf
1 large onion, chopped
15ml/1 tbsp fresh mint leaves
1 green chilli, seeded and chopped

1 In a small mixing bowl whisk together the fromage frais or crème fraîche, yogurt, orange juice, ginger, garlic, pepper, salt and coriander.

2 Pour this over the chicken and set aside for 3–4 hours.

3 Heat the oil with the bay leaf in a wok or heavy frying pan and fry the onion until soft.

4 Pour in the chicken mixture and stir-fry for 3–5 minutes over medium heat. Lower the heat, cover and cook for 7–10 minutes, adding a little water if the sauce is too thick. Add the fresh mint and chilli and serve.

NUTRITIONAL NOTES	
Per Portion	
Energy	199Kcals/836KJ
Fat	5.11g
Saturated Fat	1.06g
Carbohydrate	14.40g
Fibre	1.02g

___ COOK'S TIP ___

If you prefer the taste of curry leaves, you can use them instead of the bay leaf, but you need to double the quantity.

Fragrant Chicken Curry

In this dish, the mildly spiced sauce is thickened using low fat lentils rather than the traditional onions fried in ghee.

Ingredients

Serves 4–6

75g/3oz/½ cup red lentils
30ml/2 tbsp mild curry powder
10ml/2 tsp ground coriander
5ml/1 tsp cumin seeds
475ml/16fl oz/2 cups vegetable stock
8 chicken thigh fillets, skinned
225g/8oz fresh spinach, shredded,
  or frozen spinach, thawed and
  well drained
15ml/1 tbsp chopped fresh coriander
  (cilantro), plus extra sprigs to garnish
salt and black pepper
white or brown basmati rice and grilled
  (broiled) poppadums, to serve

1 Put the lentils in a large heavy pan with the curry powder, ground coriander, cumin seeds and vegetable stock.

2 Bring the pan to the boil, then lower the heat. Cover and simmer gently for 10 minutes.

3 Add the chicken and spinach. Replace the cover and simmer gently for a further 40 minutes, or until the chicken is cooked through.

4 Stir in the chopped coriander and season to taste. Serve garnished with fresh coriander sprigs and accompanied by white or brown basmati rice and grilled poppadums.

Nutritional Notes	
Per Portion (4)	
Energy	296Kcals/1244KJ
Fat	10.20g
Saturated Fat	2.83g
Carbohydrate	15.10g
Fibre	3.80g

——— Cook's Tip ———

Lentils are an excellent low fat source of vitamins and fibre, as well as adding subtle colour and texture to dishes. Yellow and red lentils, in particular, are very popular in Indian cooking.

Karahi Chicken with Mint

For this tasty dish, the chicken is first boiled before being quickly stir-fried in a little oil, to ensure that it is cooked through despite the short cooking time.

INGREDIENTS

Serves 4

275g/10oz chicken breast fillets, skinned and cut into strips
300ml/½ pint/1¼ cups water
30ml/2 tbsp oil
2 small bunches spring onions (scallions), roughly chopped
5ml/1 tsp shredded root ginger
5ml/1 tsp crushed dried red chillies
30ml/2 tbsp lemon juice
15ml/1 tbsp chopped fresh coriander (cilantro), plus extra sprigs to garnish
15ml/1 tbsp chopped fresh mint, plus extra sprigs to garnish
3 tomatoes, skinned, seeded and chopped
5ml/1 tsp salt

_____ COOK'S TIP _____

For a quick lunch, use the chicken as a tasty filling for warm pitta pockets or naan.

1 Put the chicken and water into a pan, bring to the boil and lower the heat to medium. Cook for about 10 minutes or until the water has evaporated and the chicken is cooked. Remove from the heat and set aside.

2 Heat the oil in a heavy frying pan or pan and stir-fry the spring onions for about 2 minutes until soft but not browned.

3 Add the boiled chicken strips and stir-fry for about 3 minutes over medium heat.

NUTRITIONAL NOTES	
Per Portion	
Energy	157Kcals/655KJ
Fat	8.20g
Saturated Fat	1.50g
Carbohydrate	4.20g
Fibre	1.40g

4 Gradually add the shredded ginger, dried red chillies, lemon juice, chopped coriander and mint, tomatoes and salt and gently stir to blend all the flavours together.

5 Transfer the spicy chicken mixture to a serving dish and garnish with a few sprigs of fresh mint and coriander before serving.

Balti Minced Chicken with Green and Red Chillies

Minced (ground) chicken is seldom cooked in Indian or Pakistani homes. However, it works very well in this recipe.

INGREDIENTS

Serves 4

275g/10oz chicken breast fillets,
    skinned and cubed
2 thick red chillies
3 thick green chillies
30ml/2 tbsp oil
6 curry leaves
3 medium onions, sliced
7.5ml/1½ tsp crushed garlic
7.5ml/1½ tsp ground coriander
7.5ml/1½ tsp crushed fresh root ginger
5ml/1 tsp chilli powder
5ml/1 tsp salt
15ml/1 tbsp lemon juice
30ml/2 tbsp chopped fresh coriander
    (cilantro)
chappatis and lemon wedges, to serve

1 Boil the chicken in water for about 10 minutes until soft and cooked through. Remove with a slotted spoon.

___ COOK'S TIP ___

Taste this dish during cooking as it is quite mild, especially if you seed the chillies, and you may find that it needs some additional spices to suit your palate.

2 Place the chicken in a food processor to mince (grind).

3 Cut the chillies in half lengthways and remove the seeds, if desired. Cut the flesh into strips and set aside.

4 Heat the oil in a wok or heavy frying pan and fry the curry leaves and onions until the onions are a soft golden brown. Lower the heat and add the garlic, ground coriander, ginger, chilli powder and salt.

5 Add the minced (ground) chicken and stir-fry for 3–5 minutes.

6 Add the lemon juice, the prepared chilli strips and most of the fresh coriander. Stir-fry for a further 3–5 minutes, then serve, garnished with the remaining fresh coriander and accompanied by warm chappatis and lemon wedges.

NUTRITIONAL NOTES	
Per Portion	
Energy	184Kcals/767KJ
Fat	8.40g
Saturated Fat	1.57g
Carbohydrate	10.10g
Fibre	1.30g

Hot Chicken Curry

This curry has a nice thick sauce, using red and green (bell) peppers for extra colour. It can be served with either warm chappatis or plain boiled rice.

Ingredients

Serves 4

30ml/2 tbsp oil
1.5ml/¼ tsp fenugreek seeds
1.5ml/¼ tsp onion seeds
2 medium onions, chopped
2.5ml/½ tsp crushed garlic
2.5ml/½ tsp crushed fresh root ginger
5ml/1 tsp ground coriander
5ml/1 tsp chilli powder
5ml/1 tsp salt
400g/14oz can tomatoes
30ml/2 tbsp lemon juice
350g/12oz chicken, skinned and cubed
30ml/2 tbsp chopped fresh coriander
  (cilantro), plus extra to garnish
3 green chillies, chopped
½ red (bell) pepper, seeded and cut
  into chunks
½ green (bell) pepper, seeded and cut
  into chunks

Nutritional Notes	
Per Portion	
Energy	214Kcals/895KJ
Fat	10.00g
Saturated Fat	2.08g
Carbohydrate	11.00g
Fibre	2.20g

1 In a medium heavy pan, heat the oil and fry the fenugreek and onion seeds until they turn a shade darker. Add the chopped onions, garlic and ginger. Fry for about 5 minutes until the onions turn golden brown. Lower the heat to very low.

2 Meanwhile, in a bowl, mix together the ground coriander, chilli powder, salt, canned tomatoes and lemon juice.

3 Pour this mixture into the pan and turn up the heat to medium. Stir-fry for about 3 minutes.

4 Add the chicken cubes and stir-fry for 5–7 minutes.

5 Add the chopped fresh coriander and green chillies and the red and green pepper chunks. Lower the heat, cover the pan and allow to simmer for about 10 minutes until the chicken cubes are cooked.

6 Serve the curry hot, garnished with fresh coriander.

COOK'S TIP

For a milder version of this delicious curry, simply omit some, or even all, of the green chillies.

Karahi Chicken with Fresh Fenugreek

Fresh fenugreek is a flavour that not many people are familiar with and this recipe is a good introduction to this delicious herb. Once again, the chicken is boiled before it is quickly stir-fried, to make sure it is cooked through.

INGREDIENTS

Serves 4

115g/4oz boneless chicken thigh fillets, skinned and cut into strips
115g/4oz chicken breast fillets, skinned and cut into strips
2.5ml/½ tsp crushed garlic
5ml/1 tsp chilli powder
2.5ml/½ tsp salt
10ml/2 tsp tomato purée (paste)
30ml/2 tbsp oil
1 bunch fenugreek leaves
15ml/1 tbsp chopped fresh coriander (cilantro)
300ml/½ pint/1¼ cups water
pilau rice and wholemeal (whole-wheat) chappatis, to serve (optional)

1 Bring a pan of water to the boil, add the chicken strips and cook for about 5–7 minutes. Drain the chicken and set aside.

2 In a mixing bowl, combine the garlic, chilli powder and salt with the tomato purée.

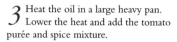

3 Heat the oil in a large heavy pan. Lower the heat and add the tomato purée and spice mixture.

4 Add the chicken pieces to the spices and stir-fry for 5–7 minutes, then lower the heat further.

5 Add the fenugreek leaves and fresh coriander. Continue to stir-fry for 5–7 minutes until all the ingredients are mixed well together.

6 Pour in the water, cover and cook for about 5 minutes until the dish is simmering. Serve hot with some pilau rice and some warm wholemeal chappatis, if wished.

NUTRITIONAL NOTES	
Per Portion	
Energy	127Kcals/528KJ
Fat	7.90g
Saturated Fat	1.51g
Carbohydrate	1.20g
Fibre	0.10g

Tandoori Chicken Kebabs

This dish originates from the plains of the Punjab at the foot of the Himalayas. There food is traditionally cooked in clay ovens known as *tandoors* – hence the name of this dish.

INGREDIENTS

Serves 4

4 chicken breast fillets, about 175g/
  6oz each, skinned
15ml/1 tbsp lemon juice
45ml/3 tbsp tandoori paste
45ml/3 tbsp natural (plain) low fat yogurt
1 garlic clove, crushed
30ml/2 tbsp chopped fresh coriander
  (cilantro), plus extra sprigs to garnish
salt and black pepper
1 small onion, cut into wedges and
  separated into layers
a little oil, for brushing
pilau rice and naan bread, to serve

NUTRITIONAL NOTES	
Per Portion	
Energy	257Kcals/1078KJ
Fat	9.40g
Saturated Fat	2.31g
Carbohydrate	3.50g
Fibre	2.90g

1 Chop the chicken breast fillets into 2.5cm/1in cubes, place in a mixing bowl and add the lemon juice, tandoori paste, yogurt, garlic, chopped coriander and seasoning. Cover and leave the chicken to marinate in the refrigerator for 2–3 hours.

2 Preheat the grill (broiler) to high. Thread alternate pieces of marinated chicken and onion on to four skewers.

3 Brush the onions with a little oil, place on a grill rack and cook under a high heat for 10–12 minutes, or until the chicken is cooked through, turning once mid-way through. Garnish the kebabs with fresh coriander sprigs and serve with pilau rice and naan bread.

_____ COOK'S TIP _____

Use chopped, boned and skinned chicken thighs, or turkey breasts, for a tasty and less expensive alternative.

Balti Chicken with Panir and Peas

This is rather an unusual combination, but it really works well. Serve with plain boiled rice.

INGREDIENTS

Serves 4

1 small chicken, about 675g/1½lb
30ml/2 tbsp tomato purée (paste)
45ml/3 tbsp natural (plain) low fat yogurt
7.5ml/1½ tsp garam masala
5ml/1 tsp crushed garlic
5ml/1 tsp crushed fresh root ginger
pinch of ground cardamom
15ml/1 tbsp chilli powder
1.5ml/¼ tsp ground turmeric
5ml/1 tsp salt
5ml/1 tsp sugar
10ml/2 tsp oil
2.5cm/1in cinnamon stick
2 black peppercorns
300ml/½ pint/1¼ cups water
115g/4oz panir, cubed
30ml/2 tbsp fresh coriander (cilantro) leaves
2 green chillies, seeded and chopped
50g/2oz low fat fromage frais or crème fraîche
75g/3oz/¾ cup frozen peas, thawed

1 Skin the chicken and cut it into 6–8 equal pieces.

_____ COOK'S TIP _____

Panir is an Indian cheese made from whole milk and provides a good source of protein.

2 Mix the tomato purée, yogurt, garam masala, crushed garlic, ginger, cardamom, chilli powder, turmeric, salt and sugar in a bowl.

3 Heat the oil with the whole spices in a wok or heavy frying pan, then pour the sauce mixture into the oil. Lower the heat and cook gently for about 3 minutes, then pour in the water and bring to a simmer.

NUTRITIONAL NOTES	
Per Portion	
Energy	233Kcals/977KJ
Fat	10.28g
Saturated Fat	4.64g
Carbohydrate	8.14g
Fibre	1.49g

4 Add the chicken pieces and stir-fry for about 2 minutes, then cover the pan and cook over medium heat for about 10 minutes.

5 Add the panir cubes to the pan, followed by half the coriander and half the green chillies. Mix well and cook for a further 5–7 minutes.

6 Stir in the fromage frais and peas, heat through and serve garnished with the reserved coriander and chillies.

Balti Chicken in a Spicy Lentil Sauce

Traditionally, this dish is made with lamb, but it is equally delicious if low fat chicken is substituted. The lentils are flavoured with a *tarka*, which is poured over the dish just before serving.

INGREDIENTS

Serves 4

30ml/2 tbsp *chana dhal*
50g/2oz/¼ cup *masoor dhal*
15ml/1 tbsp oil
2 medium onions, chopped
5ml/1 tsp crushed garlic
5ml/1 tsp crushed fresh root ginger
2.5ml/½ tsp ground turmeric
7.5ml/1½ tsp chilli powder
5ml/1 tsp garam masala
2.5ml/½ tsp ground coriander
7.5ml/1½ tsp salt
175g/6oz chicken breast fillets, skinned
   and cubed
45ml/3 tbsp fresh coriander (cilantro)
   leaves
1–2 green chillies, seeded and chopped
30-45ml/2–3 tbsp lemon juice
300ml/½ pint/1¼ cups water
2 tomatoes, peeled and halved

For the *tarka*

5ml/1 tsp oil
2.5ml/½ tsp cumin seeds
2 garlic cloves
2 dried red chillies
4 curry leaves

NUTRITIONAL NOTES	
Per Portion	
Energy	207Kcals/868KJ
Fat	7.07g
Saturated Fat	1.03g
Carbohydrate	20.37g
Fibre	2.84g

1 Boil the *chana dhal* and *masoor dhal* together in a pan of water until soft and mushy. Set aside.

2 Heat the oil in a wok or heavy frying pan and fry the onions until soft and golden brown. Stir in the garlic, ginger, turmeric, chilli powder, garam masala, ground coriander and salt.

3 Next, add the chicken pieces and stir-fry for 5–7 minutes to seal in the juices and lightly brown the meat.

4 Add half the fresh coriander, the green chillies, lemon juice and water and cook for a further 3–5 minutes before pouring in the *chana dhal* and *masoor dhal*, followed by the tomatoes.

5 Add the remaining coriander. Take off the heat and set aside.

6 To make the *tarka*, heat the oil and add the cumin seeds, whole garlic cloves, dried chillies and curry leaves. Heat for about 30 seconds and, while it is still hot, pour it over the top of the dhal. Serve immediately.

Kashmiri Chicken Curry

This mild yet flavoursome dish is given a special lift by the addition of sliced apples.

INGREDIENTS

Serves 4

10ml/2 tsp oil
2 medium onions, diced
1 bay leaf
2 cloves
2.5cm/1in cinnamon stick
4 black peppercorns
1 small chicken, about 675g/1½lb, skinned and cut into 8 pieces
5ml/1 tsp garam masala
5ml/1 tsp crushed fresh root ginger
5ml/1 tsp crushed garlic
5ml/1 tsp salt
5ml/1 tsp chilli powder
15ml/1 tbsp ground almonds
150ml/¼ pint/⅔ cup natural (plain) low fat yogurt
2 green eating apples, peeled, cored and roughly sliced
15ml/1 tbsp chopped fresh coriander (cilantro)
15g/½oz flaked (sliced) almonds, lightly toasted, and fresh coriander (cilantro) leaves, to garnish

2 Add the chicken pieces to the onions and continue to stir-fry for at least another 3 minutes.

4 Pour in the yogurt and stir for a couple more minutes.

3 Lower the heat and add the garam masala, ginger, garlic, salt, chilli powder and ground almonds and continue to stir for 2–3 minutes.

5 Add the apples and chopped coriander, cover and cook for about 10–15 minutes.

1 Heat the oil in a wok or heavy frying pan and fry the onions with the bay leaf, cloves, cinnamon and peppercorns for about 3–5 minutes until the onions are beginning to soften but are not starting to brown.

NUTRITIONAL NOTES	
Per Portion	
Energy	237Kcals/994KJ
Fat	8.25g
Saturated Fat	1.31g
Carbohydrate	17.21g
Fibre	2.88g

——————— COOK'S TIP ———————

To keep the fat content of this dish at a minimum, you could omit the ground and flaked (sliced) almonds and serve the dish with plain rice and still have a delicious meal.

6 Check that the chicken is cooked through and serve immediately, garnished with the flaked almonds and whole coriander leaves.

Balti Chicken Pieces with Cumin and Coriander

The potatoes are cooked separately in the oven before being added to the chicken. Basmati Rice with Peas and Curry Leaves is a perfect accompaniment to this dish.

INGREDIENTS

Serves 4

150ml/¼ pint/⅔ cup natural (plain) low fat yogurt
25g/1oz ground almonds
7.5ml/1½ tsp ground coriander
2.5ml/½ tsp chilli powder
5ml/1 tsp garam masala
15ml/1 tbsp coconut milk
5ml/1 tsp crushed garlic
5ml/1 tsp crushed fresh root ginger
30ml/2 tbsp chopped fresh coriander (cilantro)
1 red chilli, seeded and chopped
225g/8oz skinless chicken breast portions, boned and cubed
15ml/1 tbsp oil
2 medium onions, sliced
3 green cardamom pods
2.5cm/1in cinnamon stick
2 cloves

For the potatoes

15ml/1 tbsp oil
8 baby potatoes, thickly sliced
1.5ml/¼ tsp cumin seeds
15ml/1 tbsp finely chopped fresh coriander (cilantro)

NUTRITIONAL NOTES	
Per Portion	
Energy	2783Kcals/1166KJ
Fat	10.76g
Saturated Fat	1.58g
Carbohydrate	27.43g
Fibre	2.78g

_____ COOK'S TIP _____

Any variety of fresh mint can be added to the potatoes if you like them minty

1 In a bowl, mix together the yogurt, ground almonds, ground coriander, chilli powder, garam masala, coconut milk, garlic, ginger, half the fresh coriander and half the red chilli.

2 Place the chicken pieces in the mixture, mix well and leave to marinate for about 2 hours.

3 Meanwhile, start to prepare the potatoes. Heat the oil in a wok or heavy frying pan. Add the sliced potatoes, cumin seeds and fresh coriander and quickly stir-fry for 2–3 minutes.

4 Transfer the potatoes to a heat-proof dish, cover and cook in a preheated oven at 180°C/350°F/Gas 4 for about 30 minutes or until the potatoes are cooked through.

5 About halfway through the potatoes' cooking time, heat the oil with the onions, cardamoms, cinnamon and cloves for about 1½ minutes.

6 Add the chicken mixture to the onions and stir-fry for 5–7 minutes. Lower the heat, cover and cook for 5–7 minutes. Top with the potatoes and garnish with coriander and red chilli.

FISH AND SHELLFISH DISHES

Fish and shellfish, as well as being delicious, is naturally low in fat and cholesterol. The dishes in this section are quick to make, so are perfect for busy cooks with only limited time to spend in the kitchen. They are also very versatile and can be served with accompaniments as a main course, on their own for a nutritious evening meal, or in smaller quantities as appetizers.

Prawn Curry

A rich flavoursome curry made with prawns (shrimp) and a delicious blend of aromatic spices.

INGREDIENTS

Serves 4

675g/1½lb uncooked tiger prawns (shrimp)
4 dried red chillies
25g/1oz/½ cup desiccated (dry unsweetened shredded) coconut
5ml/1 tsp black mustard seeds
1 large onion, chopped
30ml/2 tbsp oil
4 bay leaves
2.5cm/1in piece root ginger, chopped
2 garlic cloves, crushed
15ml/1 tbsp ground coriander
5ml/1 tsp chilli powder
5ml/1 tsp salt
4 tomatoes, finely chopped
plain rice, to serve

1 Peel the prawns and discard the shells. Run a sharp knife along the centre back of each prawn to carefully remove the thin black intestinal vein.

--- COOK'S TIP ---

Serve extra tiger prawns (shrimp) unpeeled, on the edge of each plate, for an attractive garnish. Cook them with the peeled prawns (shrimp).

2 Put the dried red chillies, coconut, mustard seeds and onion in a large heavy frying pan and dry-fry for 8–10 minutes or until the spices begin to brown but not burn. Put into a food processor or blender and process to a coarse paste.

3 Heat the oil in the frying pan and fry the bay leaves for 1 minute. Add the chopped ginger and the garlic and fry for 2–3 minutes.

NUTRITIONAL NOTES	
Per Portion	
Energy	289Kcals/1212KJ
Fat	12.13g
Saturated Fat	4.18g
Carbohydrate	12.77g
Fibre	2.65g

4 Add the coriander, chilli powder, salt and the coconut paste and fry gently for 5 minutes.

5 Stir in the chopped tomatoes and about 175ml/6fl oz/¾ cup water and simmer gently for 5–6 minutes or until the sauce has thickened.

6 Add the prawns and cook for about 4–5 minutes or until they turn pink and the edges are curling slightly. Serve with plain boiled rice.

King Prawn Korma

This korma has a light, mild, creamy texture, and makes a good introduction to Indian cuisine for people who claim not to like spicy food.

INGREDIENTS

Serves 4

12–16 frozen cooked king prawns (jumbo shrimp), thawed and peeled
45ml/3 tbsp natural (plain) low fat yogurt
45ml/3 tbsp low fat fromage frais or crème fraîche
5ml/1 tsp ground paprika
5ml/1 tsp garam masala
15ml/1 tbsp tomato purée (paste)
45ml/3 tbsp coconut milk
5ml/1 tsp chilli powder
150ml/¼ pint/⅔ cup water
15ml/1 tbsp oil
5ml/1 tsp crushed garlic
5ml/1 tsp crushed fresh root ginger
½ piece cinnamon bark
2 green cardamom pods
salt
15ml/1 tbsp chopped fresh coriander (cilantro), to garnish

NUTRITIONAL NOTES	
Per Portion	
Energy	93Kcals/391KJ
Fat	4.10g
Saturated Fat	0.57g
Carbohydrate	7.20g
Fibre	0.40g

_____ COOK'S TIP _____

Paprika gives a good rich colour to the curry without adding extra heat.

1 Drain the prawns to ensure that all excess liquid is removed.

2 Place the yogurt, fromage frais, paprika, garam masala, tomato purée, coconut milk, chilli powder and water in a mixing bowl.

3 Blend all the ingredients together well and set aside.

4 Heat the oil in a wok or heavy frying pan, add the garlic, ginger, cinnamon, cardamoms and salt to taste and fry over a low heat.

5 Turn up the heat and pour in the spice mixture. Bring to the boil, stirring occasionally.

6 Add the prawns to the spices and continue to stir-fry until the sauce is quite thick. Serve garnished with the chopped fresh coriander.

Prawn and Vegetable Balti

This is a delicious accompaniment to many Indian and Balti dishes.

Ingredients

Serves 4

175g/6oz/1½ cups frozen cooked
   peeled prawns (shrimp)
30ml/2 tbsp oil
1.5ml/¼ tsp onion seeds
4-6 curry leaves
115g/4oz/1 cup frozen peas
115g/4oz/⅔ cup frozen corn
1 large courgette (zucchini), sliced
1 medium red (bell) pepper, seeded and
   roughly diced
5ml/1 tsp crushed coriander seeds
5ml/1 tsp crushed dried red chillies
1.5ml/½ tsp salt
15ml/1 tbsp lemon juice
15ml/1 tbsp fresh coriander (cilantro)
   leaves, to garnish

NUTRITIONAL NOTES	
Per Portion	
Energy	171Kcals/714KJ
Fat	7.70g
Saturated Fat	1.05g
Carbohydrate	11.8g
Fibre	2.80g

Cook's Tip

The best way to crush whole seeds is to use an electric spice grinder or a small marble mortar and pestle.

1 Thaw the prawns and drain them of any excess liquid.

2 Heat the oil with the onion seeds and curry leaves in a wok or heavy frying pan.

3 Add the prawns to the spicy mixture in the wok and stir-fry until the liquid has evaporated.

4 Next, add the peas, corn, courgette and red pepper. Continue to stir for 3–5 minutes.

5 Finally, add the crushed coriander seeds and chillies, salt to taste and the lemon juice.

6 Serve immediately, garnished with fresh coriander leaves.

Prawn and Spinach Pancakes

Serve these delicious filled pancakes hot with Spicy Baby Vegetable Salad. Try to use red onions for this recipe, although they are not essential.

INGREDIENTS

Makes 4–6 pancakes
For the pancakes
175g/6oz/1½ cups plain (all-purpose) flour
2.5ml/½ tsp salt
3 eggs
350ml/12fl oz/1½ cups semi-skimmed (low-fat) milk
15g/½oz/1 tbsp low fat margarine
1 tomato, quartered, fresh coriander (cilantro) sprigs and lemon wedges, to garnish

For the filling
30ml/2 tbsp oil
2 medium red onions, sliced
2.5ml/½ tsp crushed garlic
2.5cm/1in piece root ginger, shredded
5ml/1 tsp chilli powder
5ml/1 tsp garam masala
5ml/1 tsp salt
2 tomatoes, sliced
225g/8oz frozen leaf spinach, thawed and drained
115g/4oz/1 cup frozen cooked peeled prawns (shrimp), thawed
30ml/2 tbsp chopped fresh coriander (cilantro)

NUTRITIONAL NOTES	
Per Portion (6)	
Energy	389Kcals/1633KJ
Fat	14.70g
Saturated Fat	2.83g
Carbohydrate	48.80g
Fibre	4.00g

1 To make the pancakes, sift the flour and salt together. Beat the eggs and add to the flour, beating continuously. Gradually stir in the milk. Leave to stand for 1 hour.

2 Heat the oil in a deep frying pan and fry the sliced onions over a medium heat until golden.

3 Gradually add the garlic, ginger, chilli powder, garam masala and salt, followed by the tomatoes and spinach, stir-frying constantly.

4 Add the prawns and chopped coriander. Cook for a further 5–7 minutes or until any excess water has been absorbed. Keep warm.

5 Heat about 2.5ml/½ tsp of the low fat margarine in a 25cm/10in non-stick frying pan or pancake pan. Pour in about one-quarter of the pancake batter, tilting the pan so that the batter spreads well, coats the bottom of the pan and is evenly distributed.

6 When fine bubbles begin to appear on the surface, flip it over using a spatula and cook for a further minute or so. Transfer to a plate and keep warm. Cook the remaining pancakes in the same way.

7 Fill the pancakes with the spinach and prawns. Serve warm, garnished with the tomato, coriander sprigs and lemon wedges.

_____ COOK'S TIP _____

To keep the pancakes warm while cooking the remainder, pile them on top of each other on a plate with a sheet of greaseproof paper between each one to prevent them sticking. Place in a low oven.

Grilled King Prawn Bhoona

The unusual and delicious flavour of this dish is achieved by grilling the marinated prawns to give them a chargrilled taste and then adding them to stir-fried onions and peppers.

Ingredients

Serves 4

45ml/3 tbsp natural (plain) low fat yogurt
5ml/1 tsp paprika
5ml/1 tsp crushed fresh root ginger
salt
12–16 frozen cooked king prawns (jumbo shrimp), thawed and peeled
15ml/1 tbsp oil
3 medium onions, sliced
2.5ml/½ tsp fennel seeds, crushed
1 piece cinnamon bark
5ml/1 tsp crushed garlic
5ml/1 tsp chilli powder
1 medium yellow (bell) pepper, seeded and roughly chopped
1 medium red (bell) pepper, seeded and roughly chopped
15ml/1 tbsp fresh coriander (cilantro) leaves, to garnish

--- Cook's Tip ---

Although frozen coriander is convenient and good to use in cooking, the fresh herb is more suitable for garnishes.

Nutritional Notes	
Per Portion	
Energy	132Kcals/552KJ
Fat	3.94g
Saturated Fat	0.58g
Carbohydrate	15.95g
Fibre	3.11g

1 Blend together the yogurt, paprika, ginger and salt to taste. Pour this mixture over the prawns and leave to marinate for 30–45 minutes.

2 Meanwhile, heat the oil in a wok or heavy frying pan and fry the onions with the fennel seeds and the cinnamon bark.

3 Lower the heat and add the garlic and chilli powder.

4 Add the peppers and stir-fry gently for 3–5 minutes.

5 Remove from the heat and transfer to a warm serving dish, discarding the cinnamon bark.

6 Preheat the grill (broiler) to medium. Put the prawns in a grill pan and place under the grill to darken their tops and get a chargrilled effect. Add to the onion mixture, garnish with the coriander and serve.

King Prawns with Onion and Curry Leaves

An excellent partner for this mildly spiced prawn dish is Basmati Rice with Potato.

INGREDIENTS

Serves 4
3 medium onions
15ml/1 tbsp oil
6–8 curry leaves
1.5ml/¼ tsp onion seeds
1 green chilli, seeded and diced
1 red chilli, seeded and diced
12–16 frozen cooked king prawns
   (jumbo prawns), thawed and peeled
5ml/1 tsp shredded root ginger
5ml/1 tsp salt
15ml/1 tbsp fresh fenugreek leaves

1 Cut the onions into thin slices, using a sharp knife.

2 Heat the oil in a wok or heavy frying pan and fry the onions with the curry leaves and onion seeds for about 3 minutes.

3 Add the diced green and red chillies, followed by the prawns. Cook for about 5–7 minutes before adding the ginger and salt.

4 Finally, add the fenugreek leaves, cover and cook for a further 2–3 minutes before serving.

--- COOK'S TIP ---

For a quicker and less expensive meal, use ready-peeled small prawns (shrimp) available in most supermarkets. Allow 125g/4oz prawns per person, and cook the prawns for slightly less time than the larger ones.

NUTRITIONAL NOTES	
Per Portion	
Energy	97Kcals/403KJ
Fat	3.29g
Saturated Fat	0.45g
Carbohydrate	9.39g
Fibre	1.58g

Prawn and Mangetouts Stir-fry

It is always a good idea to keep some prawns (shrimp) in the freezer, as they are handy for a quick stir-fry like this one.

INGREDIENTS

Serves 4
15ml/1 tbsp oil
2 medium onions, diced
15ml/1 tbsp tomato purée (paste)
5ml/1 tsp Tabasco sauce
5ml/1 tsp lemon juice
5ml/1 tsp crushed fresh root ginger
5ml/1 tsp crushed garlic
5ml/1 tsp chilli powder
5ml/1 tsp salt
15ml/1 tbsp chopped fresh coriander (cilantro)
175g/6oz/1½ cups frozen cooked peeled prawns (shrimp), thawed
12 mangetouts (snow peas), halved

1 Heat the oil in a wok or heavy frying pan and fry the onions over a low heat for about 2 minutes, or until golden brown.

2 Mix the tomato purée with 30ml/2 tbsp water in a bowl. Blend in the Tabasco sauce, lemon juice, ginger and garlic pulp, chilli powder and salt.

3 Lower the heat, pour the sauce over the onions and stir-fry for a few seconds until well mixed in.

NUTRITIONAL NOTES	
Per Portion	
Energy	108Kcals/451KJ
Fat	3.48g
Saturated Fat	0.49g
Carbohydrate	7.96g
Fibre	1.60g

4 Add the coriander, prawns and mangetouts to the pan and stir-fry for 5–7 minutes, or until the sauce is thick. Serve immediately.

—— COOK'S TIP ——

Mangetouts, being small and almost flat, are perfect for stir-frying and are a popular ingredient in Indian cooking. They are particularly good stir-fried with prawns which need only minutes to heat through.

Balti Prawns with Vegetables

Tender prawns (shrimp), crunchy vegetables and a thick curry sauce combine to produce a dish rich in flavour and texture. Plain rice is a good accompaniment.

INGREDIENTS

Serves 4

30ml/2 tbsp oil
1 tsp mixed fenugreek, mustard and
   onion seeds
2 curry leaves
½ medium cauliflower, cut into
   small florets
8 baby carrots, halved lengthways
6 new potatoes, thickly sliced
50g/2 oz/½ cup frozen peas
2 medium onions, sliced
30ml/2 tbsp tomato purée (paste)
2.5ml/1½ tsp chilli powder
5ml/1 tsp ground coriander
5ml/1 tsp crushed fresh root ginger
5ml/1 tsp crushed garlic
5ml/1 tsp salt
30ml/2 tbsp lemon juice
450g/1lb frozen cooked peeled
   prawns (shrimp), thawed
30ml/2 tbsp chopped fresh coriander
   (cilantro)
1 fresh red chilli, seed and sliced
120ml/4fl oz/½ cup low fat yogurt

1 Heat the oil in a large heavy pan or wok. Lower the heat slightly and add the fenugreek, mustard and onion seeds and the curry leaves.

2 Turn up the heat and add the cauliflower, carrots, potatoes and peas. Stir-fry quickly until browned, then remove the vegetables from the pan with a slotted spoon and drain on kitchen paper.

3 Add the onions to the oil left in the pan and fry over medium heat until golden brown.

NUTRITIONAL NOTES	
Per Portion	
Energy	288Kcals/1208KJ
Fat	9.20g
Saturated Fat	1.34g
Carbohydrate	20.10g
Fibre	3.10g

4 While the onions are cooking, mix together the tomato purée, chilli powder, ground coriander, ginger, garlic, salt and lemon juice and pour the paste on to the onions.

5 Add the prawns and stir-fry over low heat for about 5 minutes or until they are heated through.

6 Add the fried vegetables to the pan and mix together well. Add the fresh coriander and red chilli and pour in the yogurt. Warm through and serve.

Stir-fried Vegetables with Monkfish

Monkfish is a rather expensive fish, but ideal to use in stir-fry recipes as it is quite tough and does not break easily.

INGREDIENTS

Serves 4
30ml/2 tbsp oil
2 medium onions, sliced
5ml/1 tsp crushed garlic
5ml/1 tsp ground cumin
5ml/1 tsp ground coriander
5ml/1 tsp chilli powder
175g/6oz monkfish, cut into cubes
30ml/2 tbsp fresh fenugreek leaves
2 tomatoes, seeded and sliced
1 courgette (zucchini), sliced
salt
15ml/1 tbsp lime juice

1 Heat the oil in a wok or heavy frying pan and fry the onions over low heat until soft.

2 Meanwhile mix together the garlic, cumin, coriander and chilli powder. Add this spice mixture to the onions and stir-fry for about 1 minute.

3 Add the fish and continue to stir-fry for 3–5 minutes until the fish is well cooked through.

4 Add the fenugreek, tomatoes and courgette, followed by salt to taste, and stir-fry for a further 2 minutes. Sprinkle with lime juice before serving.

NUTRITIONAL NOTES	
Per Portion	
Energy	86Kcals/360KJ
Fat	2.38g
Saturated Fat	0.35g
Carbohydrate	8.32g
Fibre	1.87g

_____ COOK'S TIP _____

Try to use monkfish for this recipe, but if it is not available, either cod or prawns (shrimp) make a suitable substitute.

Fish and Vegetable Kebabs

This is a very attractive dish which, served on its own, would also make an excellent appetizer for eight people.

INGREDIENTS

Serves 4

275g/10oz firm, white fish fillets, such as cod
45ml/3 tbsp lemon juice
5ml/1 tsp crushed fresh root ginger
2 green chillies, very finely chopped
15ml/1 tbsp very finely chopped fresh coriander (cilantro)
15ml/1 tbsp very finely chopped fresh mint
5ml/1 tsp ground coriander
5ml/1 tsp salt
1 red (bell) pepper
1 green (bell) pepper
½ medium cauliflower
8–10 button (white) mushrooms
8 cherry tomatoes
15ml/1 tbsp oil
1 lime, quartered, to garnish (optional)
yellow rice, to serve

NUTRITIONAL NOTES	
Per Portion	
Energy	131Kcals/551KJ
Fat	4.40g
Saturated Fat	0.51g
Carbohydrate	7.20g
Fibre	3.00g

1 Cut the fish fillets into large and even-sized chunks.

2 In a large mixing bowl, blend together the lemon juice, ginger, chopped green chillies, fresh coriander, mint, ground coriander and salt. Add the fish chunks and leave to marinate for about 30 minutes.

3 Cut the red and green peppers into large squares and divide the cauliflower into individual florets.

4 Preheat the grill (broiler) to hot. Arrange the peppers, cauliflower florets, button mushrooms and cherry tomatoes alternately with the fish pieces on four skewers.

5 Brush the kebabs with the oil and any remaining marinade. Transfer to a flameproof dish and grill (broil) for 7–10 minutes, turning occasionally, or until the fish is cooked right through.

6 Garnish with lime quarters, if wished, and serve the kebabs on a bed of yellow rice.

--- COOK'S TIP ---

Try baby corn cobs instead of mushrooms and broccoli or one of the new cultivated brassicas in place of the cauliflower.

Cod in a Tomato Sauce

The cod is lightly dusted with spices and a little cornflour (cornstarch) before being added to the tomato sauce. Mashed potatoes are the perfect accompaniment, although roast potatoes and pilau rice are also good.

INGREDIENTS

Serves 4
30ml/2 tbsp cornflour (cornstarch)
5ml/1 tsp salt
5ml/1 tsp garlic powder
5ml/1 tsp chilli powder
5ml/1 tsp ginger powder
5ml/1 tsp ground fennel seeds
5ml/1 tsp ground coriander
2 medium cod fillets, each cut
  into 2 pieces
15ml/1 tbsp oil
mashed potatoes, to serve

For the sauce

30ml/2 tbsp tomato purée (paste)
5ml/1 tsp garam masala
5ml/1 tsp chilli powder
5ml/1 tsp crushed garlic
5ml/1 tsp crushed fresh root ginger
2.5ml/½ tsp salt
175ml/6fl oz/¾ cup water
15ml/1 tbsp oil
1 bay leaf
3–4 black peppercorns
1 cm/½in piece cinnamon bark
15ml/1 tbsp chopped fresh coriander
  (cilantro)
15ml/1 tbsp chopped fresh mint

NUTRITIONAL NOTES	
Per Portion	
Energy	122Kcals/509KJ
Fat	6.65g
Saturated Fat	0.89g
Carbohydrate	4.73g
Fibre	0.48g

1 Mix together the cornflour, salt, garlic powder, chilli powder, ginger powder, ground fennel seeds and ground coriander.

2 Pour this mixture over the 4 cod pieces and make sure that they are well coated in the spices.

3 Preheat the grill (broiler) to very hot, then reduce the heat to medium and place the fish fillets under the grill. After about 5 minutes spoon the oil over the cod. Turn the cod over and repeat the process. Grill (broil) for a further 5 minutes, check that the fish is cooked through and set aside.

_____ COOK'S TIP _____

Fresh or frozen fish can be used for this dish.

4 Make the sauce by mixing together the tomato purée, garam masala, chilli powder, garlic, ginger, salt and water. Set aside.

5 Heat the oil in a wok or heavy frying pan and add the bay leaf, peppercorns and cinnamon. Pour the sauce into the wok and reduce the heat to low. Bring slowly to the boil, stirring occasionally, and simmer for about 5 minutes. Gently slide the pieces of fish into this mixture and cook for a further 2 minutes.

6 Finally, add the chopped fresh coriander and mint and serve the dish with mashed potatoes.

Green Fish Curry

This dish combines all the flavours of the East.

INGREDIENTS

Serves 4

1.5ml/¼ tsp ground turmeric
30ml/2 tbsp lime juice
pinch of salt
4 cod fillets, skinned and cut into
    5cm/2in chunks
1 onion, chopped
1 green chilli, roughly chopped
1 garlic clove, crushed
25g/1oz/¼ cup cashew nuts
2.5ml/½ tsp fennel seeds
30ml/2 tbsp desiccated (dry
    unsweetened shredded) coconut
30ml/2 tbsp oil
1.5ml/¼ tsp cumin seeds
1.5ml/¼ tsp ground coriander
1.5ml/¼ tsp ground cumin
1.5ml/¼ tsp salt
150ml/¼ pint/⅔ cup water
175ml/6fl oz/¾ cup natural (plain)
    low fat yogurt
45ml/3 tbsp finely chopped fresh
    coriander (cilantro), plus extra sprigs
    to garnish
Vegetable Pilau, to serve

1 Mix together the turmeric, lime juice and salt and rub over the fish. Cover and marinate for 15 minutes.

2 Meanwhile, process the onion, chilli, garlic, cashew nuts, fennel seeds and desiccated coconut to a paste. Spoon the paste into a bowl and set aside.

3 Heat the oil in a large heavy frying pan and fry the cumin seeds for 2 minutes or until they begin to splutter. Add the paste and fry for 5 minutes, then stir in the ground coriander, cumin, salt and water and cook for about 2–3 minutes.

4 Add the yogurt and the chopped fresh coriander. Simmer gently for 5 minutes. Add the fish fillets and gently stir in. Cover and cook gently for 10 minutes until the fish is tender. Serve with Vegetable Pilau, garnished with a coriander sprig.

NUTRITIONAL NOTES	
Per Portion	
Energy	244Kcals/1016KJ
Fat	14.30g
Saturated Fat	5.21g
Carbohydrate	5.40g
Fibre	1.70g

Indian Fish Stew

A spicy fish stew made with potatoes, peppers and traditional Indian spices.

INGREDIENTS

Serves 4

15ml/1 tbsp oil
5ml/1 tsp cumin seeds
1 onion, chopped
1 red (bell) pepper, seeded and sliced
1 garlic clove, crushed
2 red chillies, finely chopped
2 bay leaves
2.5ml/½ tsp salt
5ml/1 tsp ground cumin
5ml/1 tsp ground coriander
5ml/1 tsp chilli powder
400g/14oz can chopped tomatoes
2 large potatoes, cut into 2.5cm/ 1in chunks
300ml/½ pint/1¼ cups fish stock
4 cod fillets
chappatis, to serve

NUTRITIONAL NOTES	
Per Portion	
Energy	259Kcals/1093KJ
Fat	4.90g
Saturated Fat	0.63g
Carbohydrate	29.10g
Fibre	3.20g

2 Add the salt, ground cumin, ground coriander and chilli powder and cook for 3–4 minutes.

4 Add the fish, then cover and simmer for 10 minutes, or until the fish and potatoes are tender. Serve with warm chappatis.

1 Heat the oil in a deep heavy frying pan and fry the cumin seeds for 2 minutes until they begin to splutter. Add the onion, pepper, garlic, chillies and bay leaves and fry for 5–7 minutes until the onions have browned.

3 Stir in the tomatoes, potatoes and fish stock. Bring to the boil and simmer for a further 10 minutes.

Cod with a Spicy Mushroom Sauce

The cod is grilled (broiled) before it is added to the sauce to prevent it from breaking up during the cooking process.

Ingredients

Serves 4

4 cod fillets
15ml/1 tbsp lemon juice
15ml/1 tbsp oil
1 medium onion, chopped
1 bay leaf
4 black peppercorns, crushed
115g/4oz mushrooms
175ml/6fl oz/³/₄ cup natural (plain) low fat yogurt
5ml/1 tsp crushed fresh root ginger
5ml/1 tsp crushed garlic
2.5ml/¹/₂ tsp garam masala
2.5ml/¹/₂ tsp chilli powder
5ml/1 tsp salt
15ml/1 tbsp fresh coriander (cilantro) leaves, to garnish
lightly cooked green beans, to serve

Nutritional Notes	
Per Portion	
Energy	170Kcals/715KJ
Fat	4.32g
Saturated Fat	0.79g
Carbohydrate	7.67g
Fibre	1.00g

1 Remove the skin and any bones from the cod fillets. Sprinkle with lemon juice, then grill (broil) under a preheated grill (broiler) for about 5 minutes on each side. Remove the fillets from the heat and set aside.

2 Heat the oil in a wok or heavy frying pan and fry the onion with the bay leaf and peppercorns for 2–3 minutes. Lower the heat, then add the whole mushrooms and stir-fry for a further 4–5 minutes.

--- Cook's Tip ---

If you can find tiny button (white) mushrooms they look very attractive in this fish dish. Alternatively, choose from the many other pretty coloured varieties, such as ceps and oyster mushrooms.

3 In a bowl mix together the yogurt, ginger and garlic, garam masala, chilli and salt. Pour this over the onions and stir-fry for 3 minutes.

4 Add the cod fillets to the sauce and cook for a further 2 minutes. Serve garnished with the fresh coriander and accompanied by lightly cooked green beans.

Spicy Grilled Fish Fillets

The nice thing about fish is that it can be cooked beautifully without sacrificing any flavour.

INGREDIENTS

Serves 4

4 medium flatfish fillets, such as
   plaice, sole or flounder, about
   115g/4oz each
5ml/1 tsp crushed garlic
5ml/1 tsp garam masala
5ml/1 tsp chilli powder
1.5ml/¼ tsp ground turmeric
2.5ml/½ tsp salt
15ml/1 tbsp finely chopped fresh
   coriander (cilantro)
15ml/1 tbsp oil
30ml/2 tbsp lemon juice
tomato wedges, lime slices and grated
   carrot, to garnish

1 Line a flameproof dish or grill pan with foil. Rinse and pat dry the fish fillets and put them in the foil-lined dish or pan.

2 In a bowl, mix the garlic, garam masala, chilli powder, turmeric, salt, coriander, oil and lemon juice.

3 Brush the fish fillets evenly all over with the spice mixture.

4 Preheat the grill (broiler) to very hot, then lower the heat to medium. Grill (broil) the fish for about 10 minutes, basting with the spice mixture, until it is cooked right through.

5 Serve immediately with a garnish of tomato wedges, lime slices and grated carrot.

NUTRITIONAL NOTES	
Per Portion	
Energy	152Kcals/641KJ
Fat	5.90g
Saturated Fat	0.88g
Carbohydrate	3.70g
Fibre	0.70g

——— COOK'S TIP ———

Use lime juice instead of lemon to give the dish a slightly more sour flavour.

Tuna Fish Curry

This unusual fish curry can be made in minutes.

INGREDIENTS

Serves 4
1 onion
1 red (bell) pepper
1 green (bell) pepper
30ml/2 tbsp oil
1.5ml/¼ tsp cumin seeds
2.5ml/½ tsp ground cumin
2.5ml/½ tsp ground coriander
2.5ml/½ tsp chilli powder
1.5ml/¼ tsp salt
2 garlic cloves, crushed
400g/14oz can tuna in brine, drained
1 green chilli, finely chopped
2.5cm/1in piece root ginger, grated
1.5ml/¼ tsp garam masala
5ml/1 tsp lemon juice
30ml/2 tbsp chopped fresh coriander
   (cilantro), plus extra sprig, to garnish
pitta bread and Cucumber Raita,
   to serve

_____ COOK'S TIP _____

Place the pitta bread on a grill (broiler) rack and grill (broil) until it just puffs up. It will then be easy to split with a sharp knife.

NUTRITIONAL NOTES	
Per Portion	
Energy	165Kcals/690KJ
Fat	6.80g
Saturated Fat	0.97g
Carbohydrate	8.70g
Fibre	1.80g

1 Thinly slice the onion and the red and green peppers, discarding the seeds from the peppers.

2 Heat the oil in a large heavy frying pan and stir-fry the cumin seeds for 2–3 minutes until they begin to spit and splutter.

3 Add the ground cumin, coriander, chilli powder and salt and cook for 2–3 minutes. Then add the garlic, onion and peppers.

4 Fry the vegetables, stirring from time to time, for 5–7 minutes until the onion has browned.

5 Stir in the tuna, green chilli and ginger and cook for 5 minutes.

6 Add the garam masala, lemon juice and chopped fresh coriander and continue to cook the curry for a further 3–4 minutes. Serve in warmed, split pitta bread with the Cucumber Raita, garnished with a coriander sprig.

Fish and Okra Curry

An interesting combination of flavours and textures is used in this delicious fish dish.

INGREDIENTS

Serves 4

450g/1lb monkfish
5ml/1 tsp ground turmeric
2.5ml/½ tsp chilli powder
2.5ml/½ tsp salt
5ml/1 tsp cumin seeds
2.5ml/½ tsp fennel seeds
2 dried red chillies
30ml/2 tbsp oil
1 onion, finely chopped
2 garlic cloves, crushed
4 tomatoes, peeled and finely chopped
150ml/¼ pint/⅔ cup water
225g/8oz okra, trimmed and cut into
    2.5cm/1in lengths
5ml/1 tsp garam masala
plain rice, to serve

1 Remove the membrane and bones from the monkfish, cut into 2.5cm/1in cubes and place in a dish. Mix together the turmeric, chilli powder and 1.5ml/¼ tsp of the salt and rub the mixture all over the fish. Marinate for 15 minutes.

_____ COOK'S TIP _____

Yellow and plain rice would also go very well with this fish curry, making a very attractive presentation. Or serve it with plain rice, if you prefer.

2 Put the cumin seeds, fennel seeds and chillies in a large heavy frying pan and dry-roast the spices for 3–4 minutes. Put the spices into a blender or use a mortar and pestle and grind to a coarse powder.

3 Heat 15ml/1 tbsp of the oil in the frying pan and fry the monkfish cubes for about 4–5 minutes. Remove with a slotted spoon and drain on kitchen paper.

NUTRITIONAL NOTES	
Per Portion	
Energy	193Kcals/805KJ
Fat	8.80g
Saturated Fat	1.31g
Carbohydrate	9.40g
Fibre	3.60g

4 Add the remaining oil to the pan and fry the onion and garlic for about 5 minutes. Add the roasted spice powder and remaining salt and fry for 2–3 minutes. Stir in the tomatoes and water and simmer for 5 minutes.

5 Add the prepared okra and cook for about 5–7 minutes.

6 Return the fish to the pan together with the garam masala. Cover and simmer for 5–6 minutes or until the fish is tender. Serve at once with plain rice.

Fish Fillets with a Chilli Sauce

For this recipe, the fish fillets are first marinated with fresh coriander and lemon juice, then cooked under a hot grill (broiler) and served with a chilli sauce.

INGREDIENTS

Serves 4

4 flatfish fillets, such as plaice, sole
  or flounder, about 115g/4oz each
30ml/2 tbsp lemon juice
15ml/1 tbsp finely chopped
  fresh coriander (cilantro)
15ml/1 tbsp oil
lime wedges and a fresh coriander
  (cilantro) sprig, to garnish
yellow rice, to serve

For the sauce

5ml/1 tsp crushed fresh root ginger
30ml/2 tbsp tomato purée (paste)
5ml/1 tsp sugar
5ml/1 tsp salt
15ml/1 tbsp chilli sauce
15ml/1 tbsp malt vinegar
300ml/½ pint/1¼ cups water

NUTRITIONAL NOTES	
Per Portion	
Energy	149Kcals/627KJ
Fat	5.40g
Saturated Fat	0.81g
Carbohydrate	3.90g
Fibre	0.20g

COOK'S TIP

Chopped fresh coriander (cilantro) and lemon juice are popular marinade ingredients for Indian fish dishes. For a subtle change in flavour, you can substitute an equal quantity of lime juice for the lemon juice in the marinade, and then garnish the dish with lemon wedges rather than lime.

1 Rinse and pat dry the fish fillets and place in a medium bowl. Add the lemon juice, coriander and oil and rub into the fish. Leave to marinate for at least 1 hour.

2 Mix together all the sauce ingredients in a bowl, pour into a small pan and simmer gently over low heat for about 6 minutes, stirring occasionally.

3 Preheat the grill (broiler) to medium. Place the fish fillets under the grill (broil) for about 5–7 minutes.

4 When the fish is cooked, arrange it on a warmed serving dish.

5 The chilli sauce should now be fairly thick – about the consistency of a thick chicken soup.

6 Pour the sauce over the fish fillets, garnish with the lime wedges and coriander sprig and serve immediately with yellow rice.

VEGETABLE DISHES

Everyone should eat fresh vegetables regularly for good health, and with the ever-increasing range of produce now available all the year round there is no excuse for not serving a vegetable accompaniment with all your meals. These delicately spiced recipes will complement any of the other dishes in this book, or they can be eaten as a appetizer, or a combination can be eaten for a delicious vegetarian meal.

Mixed Vegetable Curry

A good all-round vegetable curry that goes well with most Indian meat dishes. You can use any combination of vegetables that are in season for this basic recipe.

INGREDIENTS

Serves 4

15ml/1 tbsp oil
2.5ml/½ tsp black mustard seeds
2.5ml/½ tsp cumin seeds
1 onion, thinly sliced
2 curry leaves
1 green chilli, finely chopped
2.5cm/1in piece root ginger,
   finely chopped
30ml/2 tbsp curry paste
1 small cauliflower, broken into florets
1 large carrot, thickly sliced
115g/4oz green beans, cut into
   2.5cm/1in lengths
1.5ml/¼ tsp ground turmeric
1.5ml/¼ tsp chilli powder
2.5ml/½ tsp salt
2 tomatoes, finely chopped
50g/2oz/½ cup frozen peas, thawed
150ml/¼ pint/⅔ cup vegetable stock
fresh curry leaves, to garnish

NUTRITIONAL NOTES	
Per Portion	
Energy	130Kcals/540KJ
Fat	6.20g
Saturated Fat	0.61g
Carbohydrate	12.30g
Fibre	6.20g

_____ COOK'S TIP _____

To turn this dish into a non-vegetarian main course, add some prawns (shrimp) or cubes of cooked chicken with the stock.

1 Heat the oil in a large heavy pan and fry the mustard seeds and cumin seeds for 2 minutes until they begin to splutter.

2 Add the onion and the curry leaves and fry for 5 minutes.

3 Add the chilli and ginger and fry for 2 minutes. Stir in the curry paste and fry for 3–4 minutes.

4 Add the cauliflower florets, sliced carrot and green beans and cook for 4–5 minutes. Add the turmeric, chilli powder, salt and tomatoes and cook for 2–3 minutes.

5 Add the thawed peas and cook for a further 2–3 minutes.

6 Add the stock. Cover and simmer over a low heat for 10–15 minutes until all the vegetables are tender. Serve garnished with curry leaves.

Courgette Curry

Thickly sliced courgettes are combined with authentic Indian spices for a tasty and colourful vegetable curry.

Ingredients

Serves 4

675g/1½lb courgettes (zucchini)
30ml/2 tbsp oil
2.5ml/½ tsp cumin seeds
2.5ml/½ tsp mustard seeds
1 onion, thinly sliced
2 garlic cloves, crushed
1.5ml/¼ tsp ground turmeric
1.5ml/¼ tsp chilli powder
5ml/1 tsp ground coriander
5ml/1 tsp ground cumin
2.5ml/½ tsp salt
15ml/1 tbsp tomato purée (paste)
400g/14oz can chopped tomatoes
150ml/¼ pint/⅔ cup water
15ml/1 tbsp chopped fresh coriander (cilantro)
5ml/1 tsp garam masala

1 Trim the ends from the courgettes then cut them evenly into 1cm/½in thick slices.

_____ Cook's Tip _____

You can use medium-sized courgettes (zucchini) or the slightly larger ones for this dish. Whichever size you choose, look for smooth, shiny ones without blemishes.

2 Heat the oil in a large heavy pan and fry the cumin and mustard seeds for 2 minutes until they begin to splutter.

3 Add the onion and garlic and fry for about 5–6 minutes.

4 Add the turmeric, chilli powder, ground coriander, cumin and salt and fry for about 2–3 minutes.

5 Add the sliced courgettes all at once, and cook for 5 minutes, stirring so they do not burn.

6 Mix together the tomato purée and chopped tomatoes and add to the pan with the water. Cover and simmer for 10 minutes until the sauce thickens. Stir in the fresh coriander and garam masala, then cook for 5 minutes or until the courgettes are tender.

Nutritional Notes	
Per Portion	
Energy	133Kcals/550KJ
Fat	7.20g
Saturated Fat	0.91g
Carbohydrate	11.60g
Fibre	2.80g

Vegetable Kashmiri

This is a wonderful vegetable curry, in which fresh mixed vegetables are cooked in a spicy aromatic yogurt sauce.

Ingredients

Serves 4

10ml/2 tsp cumin seeds
8 black peppercorns
2 green cardamom pods, seeds only
5cm/2in cinnamon stick
2.5ml/½ tsp grated nutmeg
30ml/2 tbsp oil
1 green chilli, chopped
2.5cm/1in piece root ginger, grated
5ml/1 tsp chilli powder
2.5ml/½ tsp salt
2 large potatoes, cut into 2.5cm/
 1in chunks
225g/8oz cauliflower, broken
 into florets
225g/8oz okra, trimmed and
 thickly sliced
150ml/¼ pint/⅔ cup natural (plain)
 low fat yogurt
150ml/¼ pint/⅔ cup vegetable stock
toasted flaked (sliced) almonds
 (optional) and fresh coriander
 (cilantro) sprigs, to garnish

1 Grind the cumin seeds, peppercorns, cardamom seeds, cinnamon stick and nutmeg to a fine powder using a coffee blender or a mortar and pestle.

2 Heat the oil in a large heavy pan and fry the chilli powder and ginger for 2 minutes, stirring all the time.

3 Add the chilli powder, salt and ground spice mixture and fry for about 2–3 minutes, stirring all the time to prevent the spices from sticking.

Nutritional Notes	
Per Portion	
Energy	220Kcals/920KJ
Fat	8.20g
Saturated Fat	1.02g
Carbohydrate	29.10g
Fibre	4.70g

——————— Cook's Tip ———————

Instead of the vegetable mixture used here, try cooking other ones of your choice in this lovely yogurt sauce.

4 Stir in the potatoes, cover and cook for 10 minutes over low heat, stirring from time to time.

5 Add the cauliflower and okra and cook for 5 minutes.

6 Add the yogurt and stock. Bring to the boil, then reduce the heat. Cover and simmer for 20 minutes, or until all the vegetables are tender. Garnish with toasted almonds, if using, and coriander sprigs.

Stuffed Baby Vegetables

The combination of potatoes and aubergines is popular in Indian cooking. This recipe uses small vegetables, which are stuffed with a dry, spicy masala paste.

INGREDIENTS

Serves 4
12 small potatoes
8 baby aubergines (eggplants)

For the stuffing
15ml/1 tbsp sesame seeds
30ml/2 tbsp ground coriander
30ml/2 tbsp ground cumin
2.5ml/½ tsp salt
1.5ml/¼ tsp chilli powder
2.5ml/½ tsp ground turmeric
10ml/2 tsp sugar
1.5ml/¼ tsp garam masala
15ml/1 tbsp gram flour
2 garlic cloves, crushed
15ml/1 tbsp lemon juice
30ml/2 tbsp chopped fresh coriander
   (cilantro)

For the sauce
15ml/1 tbsp oil
2.5ml/½ tsp black mustard seeds
400g/14oz can chopped tomatoes
30ml/2 tbsp chopped fresh coriander
   (cilantro)
150ml/¼ pint/⅔ cup water

1 Preheat the oven to 200°C/400°F/ Gas 6. Make slits in the potatoes and aubergines, ensuring that you do not cut right through.

2 Mix all the ingredients for the stuffing together on a plate.

3 Carefully spoon the spicy stuffing mixture into each of the slits in the potatoes and aubergines.

4 Arrange the stuffed potatoes and aubergines in a greased ovenproof dish, filling side up.

_____ Cook's Tip _____

Make sure that the potatoes are all about the same size and the baby aubergines (egg-plants) are a similar size, so that they all cook evenly.

5 For the sauce, heat the oil in a heavy pan and fry the mustard seeds for 2 minutes until they begin to splutter, then add the canned tomatoes, chopped coriander and any leftover stuffing together with the water. Bring to the boil and simmer for 5 minutes until the sauce thickens.

6 Pour the sauce over the potatoes and aubergines. Cover and bake in the oven for 25–30 minutes until the potatoes and aubergines are soft.

NUTRITIONAL NOTES	
Per Portion	
Energy	259Kcals/1088KJ
Fat	7.60g
Saturated Fat	0.73g
Carbohydrate	41.30g
Fibre	4.00g

Aubergine Curry

A simple and delicious way of cooking aubergines which retains their full flavour.

INGREDIENTS

Serves 4

2 large aubergines (eggplants), about
    450g/1lb each
15ml/1 tbsp oil
2.5ml/½ tsp black mustard seeds
1 bunch spring onions (scallions), finely
    chopped
115g/4oz/1½ cups button (white)
    mushrooms, halved
2 garlic cloves, crushed
1 red chilli, finely chopped
2.5ml/½ tsp chilli powder
5ml/1 tsp ground cumin
5ml/1 tsp ground coriander
1.5ml/¼ tsp ground turmeric
5ml/1 tsp salt
400g/14oz can chopped tomatoes
15ml/1 tbsp chopped fresh coriander
    (cilantro), plus extra sprig, to garnish

1 Preheat the oven to 200°C/400°F/
Gas 6. Wrap the aubergines
individually in foil and bake in the oven
for 1 hour or until soft. Remove and
unwrap. Allow to cool.

NUTRITIONAL NOTES	
Per Portion	
Energy	99Kcals/413KJ
Fat	4.60g
Saturated Fat	0.45g
Carbohydrate	10.40g
Fibre	6.00g

2 Meanwhile, heat the oil in a heavy
pan and fry the mustard seeds for
2 minutes until they begin to splutter.
Add the spring onions, mushrooms,
garlic and chilli and fry for 5 minutes.
Stir in the chilli powder, cumin,
ground coriander, turmeric and salt
and fry for 3–4 minutes. Add the
tomatoes and simmer for 5 minutes.

──────── COOK'S TIP ────────

This curry can be served as a vegetarian
main course or as an accompaniment to a
lamb or chicken dish. If preferred, you can
use four large courgettes (zucchini) in place
of the aubergines (eggplants) used here.

3 Cut each of the aubergines in half
lengthways and scoop out the
soft flesh into a mixing bowl. Mash the
flesh roughly with a fork.

4 Add the mashed aubergines and
chopped fresh coriander to the
pan. Bring to the boil and simmer
for 5 minutes or until the sauce
thickens. Serve garnished with a fresh
coriander sprig.

Mushroom Curry

This is a delicious way of cooking mushrooms which goes well with meat dishes, such as Spicy Lamb and Potato Stew.

INGREDIENTS

Serves 4
30ml/2 tbsp oil
2.5ml/¹⁄₂ tsp cumin seeds
1.5ml/¹⁄₄ tsp black peppercorns
4 green cardamom pods
1.5ml/¹⁄₄ tsp ground turmeric
1 onion, finely chopped
5ml/1 tsp ground cumin
5ml/1 tsp ground coriander
2.5ml/¹⁄₂ tsp garam masala
1 green chilli, finely chopped
2 garlic cloves, crushed
2.5cm/1in piece root ginger, grated
400g/14oz can chopped tomatoes
1.5ml/¹⁄₄ tsp salt
450g/1lb button (white) mushrooms, halved
chopped fresh coriander (cilantro), to garnish

NUTRITIONAL NOTES	
Per Portion	
Energy	113Kcals/469KJ
Fat	6.90g
Saturated Fat	0.88g
Carbohydrate	8.80g
Fibre	2.50g

_____ COOK'S TIP _____

The distinctive flavour of mushrooms goes well with this mixture of spices. If you don't want to use button mushrooms, you can substitute any other mushrooms.

1 Heat the oil in a large heavy pan and fry the cumin seeds, peppercorns, cardamom pods and turmeric for 2–3 minutes.

2 Add the onion and fry for about 5 minutes until golden. Stir in the cumin, ground coriander and garam masala and fry for a further 2 minutes.

3 Add the chilli, garlic and ginger and fry for 2–3 minutes, stirring all the time to prevent the spices from sticking to the pan. Add the tomatoes and salt. Bring to the boil and simmer for 5 minutes.

4 Add the mushrooms. Cover and simmer over a low heat for 10 minutes. Garnish with chopped fresh coriander before serving.

Balti Stir-fried Vegetables with Cashew Nuts

This quick and versatile stir-fry
will accommodate most other
combinations of vegetables – you
do not have to use the selection
suggested here.

INGREDIENTS

Serves 4

2 medium carrots
1 medium red (bell) pepper, seeded
1 medium green (bell) pepper, seeded
2 courgettes (zucchini)
115g/4oz green beans
1 medium bunch spring onions
    (scallions)
15ml/1 tbsp oil
4–6 curry leaves
2.5ml/½ tsp cumin seeds
4 dried red chillies
10–12 cashew nuts
5ml/1 tsp salt
30ml/2 tbsp lemon juice
fresh mint leaves, to garnish

1 Prepare the vegetables: cut the
carrots, peppers and courgettes
into matchsticks, halve the beans and
chop the spring onions. Set aside.

NUTRITIONAL NOTES	
Per Portion	
Energy	98Kcals/406KJ
Fat	5.28g
Saturated Fat	0.88g
Carbohydrate	10.36g
Fibre	3.94g

2 Heat the oil in a wok or heavy
pan and fry the curry leaves,
cumin seeds and dried chillies for
about 1 minute.

3 Add the vegetables and nuts and
stir them around gently. Add the
salt and lemon juice. Continue to stir
and cook for about 3–5 minutes.

4 Transfer the vegetables to a serving
dish, garnish with fresh mint leaves
and serve immediately.

COOK'S TIP

If you are short of time, substitute frozen
mixed vegetables for the carrots, (bell)
peppers, courgettes (zucchini) and green
beans; they work equally well in this dish.

Broad Beans and Cauliflower Curry

This is a hot and spicy vegetable curry, ideal when served with cooked rice (especially a brown basmati variety), small poppadums and perhaps a cooling Cucumber Raita as well.

INGREDIENTS

Serves 4

2 garlic cloves, chopped
2.5cm/1in piece root ginger
1 fresh green chilli, seeded and chopped
30ml/2 tbsp oil
1 onion, sliced
1 large potato, chopped
15ml/1 tbsp curry powder, mild or hot
1 cauliflower, cut into small florets
600ml/1 pint/2½ cups stock
salt and black pepper
275g/10oz can broad (fava) beans, and liquor
juice of ½ lemon (optional)
fresh coriander (cilantro) sprig, to garnish
plain rice, to serve

1 Blend the garlic, ginger, chilli and 15ml/1 tbsp of the oil in a food processor or blender until the mixture forms a smooth paste.

2 In a large heavy pan, fry the onion and potato in the remaining oil for 5 minutes, then stir in the spice paste and curry powder. Cook for another minute.

3 Add the cauliflower florets to the onion and potato and stir well until they are thoroughly combined with the spicy mixture, then pour in the stock and bring to the boil.

4 Season well, cover and simmer for 10 minutes. Add the beans and their liquor and cook, uncovered, for a further 10 minutes.

5 Check the seasoning and adjust if necessary. Add a good squeeze of lemon juice, if liked, and serve hot, garnished with coriander and accompanied by plain boiled rice.

_____ COOK'S TIP _____

Other root vegetables, such as parsnips and carrots, can be used in this recipe.

NUTRITIONAL NOTES	
Per Portion	
Energy	216Kcals/906KJ
Fat	7.70g
Saturated Fat	0.75g
Carbohydrate	25.80g
Fibre	7.90g

Masala Beans with Fenugreek

"Masala" means spice and this vegetarian dish is spicy.

Ingredients

Serves 4

5ml/1 tsp ground cumin
5ml/1 tsp ground coriander
5ml/1 tsp sesame seeds
5ml/1 tsp chilli powder
1.5ml/¼ tsp ground turmeric
5ml/1 tsp salt
2.5ml/½ tsp crushed garlic
1 medium onion, roughly chopped
15ml/1 tbsp oil
1 tomato, quartered
225g/8oz green beans
1 bunch fresh fenugreek leaves,
   stems discarded
60ml/4 tbsp chopped fresh coriander
   (cilantro)
15ml/1 tbsp lemon juice

1 Mix together the ground cumin and coriander, sesame seeds, chilli powder, turmeric and salt.

2 Stir the crushed garlic into the dry spices, then place all of these ingredients in a food processor with the roughly chopped onion. Process for about 30–45 seconds until the mixture forms a thick creamy paste.

3 In a medium heavy pan, heat the oil and fry the spice mixture for about 5 minutes, stirring occasionally.

4 Add the tomato, green beans, fenugreek and fresh coriander.

5 Stir-fry the bean mixture for about 5 minutes, sprinkle in the lemon juice and serve immediately.

Nutritional Notes	
Per Portion	
Energy	79Kcals/327KJ
Fat	4.50g
Saturated Fat	0.56g
Carbohydrate	7.00g
Fibre	2.00g

Spinach with Mushrooms and Red Pepper

A tasty and nutritious vegetable, spinach cooked in this way is wonderful served with chappatis.

INGREDIENTS

Serves 4

450g/1lb fresh or frozen spinach
30ml/2 tbsp oil
2 medium onions, diced
6–8 curry leaves
1.5ml/¼ tsp onion seeds
5ml/1 tsp crushed garlic
5ml/1 tsp crushed fresh root ginger
5ml/1 tsp chilli powder
5ml/1 tsp salt
7.5ml/1½ tsp ground coriander
1 large red (bell) pepper, seeded and sliced
115g/4oz/1½ cups mushrooms, roughly chopped
225g/8oz/1 cup low fat fromage frais or crème fraîche
30ml/2 tbsp fresh coriander (cilantro) leaves

1 If using fresh spinach, blanch it briefly in boiling water and drain thoroughly. If using frozen spinach, thaw first, then drain. Set aside.

NUTRITIONAL NOTES	
Per Portion	
Energy	188Kcals/778KJ
Fat	11.57g
Saturated Fat	5.99g
Carbohydrate	14.71g
Fibre	4.68g

2 Heat the oil in a wok or heavy frying pan and fry the onions with the curry leaves and the onion seeds for 1–2 minutes. Add the garlic, ginger, chilli powder, salt and ground coriander. Stir-fry for a further 2–3 minutes.

3 Add half the red pepper slices and all the mushrooms and continue to stir-fry for 2–3 minutes.

4 Add the spinach and stir-fry for 4–6 minutes, then add the fromage frais or crème fraîche and half the fresh coriander, followed by the remaining red pepper slices. Stir-fry for a further 2–3 minutes before serving, garnished with the remaining coriander.

_____ COOK'S TIP _____

Whether you use fresh or frozen spinach, make sure it is well drained, otherwise the stir-fried mixture will be too wet when you add the fromage frais or crème fraîche.

Okra in Yogurt

This tangy vegetable dish can be served as an accompaniment, but it also makes an excellent vegetarian meal if served with *Tarka Dhal* and warm, freshly made chappatis.

INGREDIENTS

Serves 4
450g/1lb okra
15ml/1 tbsp oil
2.5ml/½ tsp onion seeds
3 medium green chillies, chopped
1 medium onion, sliced
1.5ml/¼ tsp turmeric
2.5ml/½ tsp salt
15ml/1 tbsp natural (plain) low fat yogurt
2 medium tomatoes, sliced
15ml/1 tbsp chopped fresh coriander
   (cilantro)
chappatis, to serve

NUTRITIONAL NOTES	
Per Portion	
Energy	82Kcals/342KJ
Fat	4.20g
Saturated Fat	0.41g
Carbohydrate	7.60g
Fibre	5.30g

1 Wash, top and tail the okra, cut into 1cm/½in pieces and set aside.

2 Heat the oil in a medium heavy frying pan, add the onion seeds, chillies and onion and fry for about 5 minutes until the onion has turned golden brown.

3 Lower the heat and add the turmeric and salt to the onions and fry for about 1 minute.

4 Next, add the prepared okra, turn the heat to medium-high and quickly stir-fry the okra for a few minutes until they are lightly golden.

5 Add the yogurt, tomatoes and, finally, the coriander. Cook for a further 2 minutes.

6 Transfer the okra to a serving dish and serve immediately with freshly made chappatis.

Aloo Gobi

Cauliflower and potatoes are encrusted with Indian spices in this delicious recipe.

INGREDIENTS

Serves 4
450g/1lb potatoes, cut into 2.5cm/
   1in chunks
30ml/2 tbsp oil
5ml/1 tsp cumin seeds
1 green chilli, finely chopped
450g/1lb cauliflower, broken into florets
5ml/1 tsp ground coriander
5ml/1 tsp ground cumin
1.5ml/¼ tsp chilli powder
2.5ml/½ tsp ground turmeric
2.5ml/½ tsp salt
chopped fresh coriander (cilantro),
   to garnish
tomato and onion salad and pickle,
   to serve

1 Par-boil the potatoes in a large pan of boiling water for 10 minutes. Drain well and set aside.

2 Heat the oil in a large heavy frying pan and fry the cumin seeds for 2 minutes until they begin to splutter. Add the chilli and fry for a further 1 minute.

3 Add the cauliflower florets and fry, stirring, for 5 minutes.

4 Add the potatoes and the ground spices and salt and cook for a further 7–10 minutes, or until both the vegetables are tender. Garnish with fresh coriander and serve with tomato and onion salad and pickle.

NUTRITIONAL NOTES	
Per Portion	
Energy	189Kcals/791KJ
Fat	7.40g
Saturated Fat	0.77g
Carbohydrate	24.60g
Fibre	3.50g

_____ COOK'S TIP _____

Use sweet potatoes instead of ordinary potatoes for a curry with a sweeter flavour.

Aloo Saag

Spinach, potatoes and traditional
Indian spices are the main
ingredients in this simple but
authentic curry.

INGREDIENTS

Serves 4

450g/1lb spinach
15ml/1 tbsp oil
5ml/1 tsp black mustard seeds
1 onion, thinly sliced
2 garlic cloves, crushed
2.5cm/1in piece root ginger,
  finely chopped
675g/1½lb potatoes, cut into
  2.5cm/1in chunks
5ml/1 tsp chilli powder
5ml/1 tsp salt
120ml/4fl oz/½ cup water

NUTRITIONAL NOTES	
Per Portion	
Energy	203Kcals/851KJ
Fat	4.60g
Saturated Fat	0.65g
Carbohydrate	34.40g
Fibre	5.10g

COOK'S TIP

To make certain that the spinach is
completely dry, put it in a clean dish towel,
roll up tightly and squeeze gently to
remove any excess liquid. Use a waxy
variety of potato for this dish so that the
pieces do not break up during cooking.

1 Wash and trim the spinach, then
blanch it in a pan of boiling water
for about 3–4 minutes.

2 Drain the spinach thoroughly and
set aside. When it is cool enough
to handle, use your hands to squeeze
out any remaining liquid (see Cook's
Tip) and set aside.

3 Heat the oil in a large heavy pan
and fry the mustard seeds for 2
minutes or until they splutter.

4 Add the sliced onion, garlic cloves
and chopped ginger to the mustard
seeds and fry for 5 minutes, stirring.

5 Add the potato chunks, chilli
powder, salt and water and stir-fry
for a further 8 minutes.

6 Add the drained spinach. Cover
the pan with a lid and simmer for
10–15 minutes or until the potatoes
are tender. Serve hot.

Masala Okra

Okra, or "ladies' fingers", are a very popular Indian vegetable. In this recipe they are stir-fried with a dry masala mixture to make a tasty side dish.

INGREDIENTS

Serves 4

450g/1lb okra
2.5ml/½ tsp ground turmeric
5ml/1 tsp chilli powder
15ml/1 tbsp ground cumin
15ml/1 tbsp ground coriander
1.5ml/¼ tsp salt
1.5ml/¼ tsp sugar
15ml/1 tbsp lemon juice
30ml/2 tbsp chopped fresh coriander
(cilantro)
15ml/1 tbsp oil
2.5ml/½ tsp cumin seeds
2.5ml/½ tsp black mustard seeds
chopped fresh tomatoes, to garnish
poppadums, to serve

1 Wash, dry and trim the okra and set aside. In a bowl, mix together the turmeric, chilli powder, cumin, ground coriander, salt, sugar, lemon juice and fresh coriander.

--- COOK'S TIP ---

When buying okra, choose firm, brightly coloured pods that are less than 10cm/4in long; larger ones can be stringy.

2 Heat the oil in a large heavy frying pan. Add the cumin seeds and mustard seeds and fry for about 2 minutes or until they splutter.

3 Add the spice mixture and continue to fry for 2 minutes.

4 Add the okra, cover and cook over a low heat for 10 minutes, or until tender. Garnish with chopped fresh tomatoes and serve with poppadums.

NUTRITIONAL NOTES	
Per Portion	
Energy	102Kcals/424KJ
Fat	5.40g
Saturated Fat	0.44g
Carbohydrate	8.60g
Fibre	4.70g

Spicy Bitter Gourds

Bitter gourds are widely used in Indian cooking, often combined with other vegetables in a curry.

INGREDIENTS

Serves 4

675g/1½lb bitter gourds
15ml/1 tbsp oil
2.5ml/½ tsp cumin seeds
6 spring onions (scallions), chopped
5 tomatoes, finely chopped
2.5cm/1in piece root ginger, chopped
2 garlic cloves, crushed
2 green chillies, finely chopped
2.5ml/½ tsp salt
2.5ml/½ tsp chilli powder
5ml/1 tsp ground coriander
5ml/1 tsp ground cumin
45ml/3 tbsp soft dark brown sugar
15ml/1 tbsp gram flour
fresh coriander (cilantro) sprigs, to
   garnish

1 Bring a large pan of lightly salted water to the boil. Peel the bitter gourds using a small sharp knife and halve them. Discard the seeds. Cut into 2cm/¾in pieces, then cook in the boiling water for about 10–15 minutes or until they are just tender. Drain well and set aside.

2 Heat the oil in a large heavy pan and fry the cumin seeds for 2 minutes until they begin to splutter. Add the spring onions and fry for 3–4 minutes. Add the tomatoes, ginger, garlic and chillies and cook for a further 5 minutes.

3 Add the salt, remaining spices and sugar to the pan and cook for a further 2–3 minutes.

4 Add the bitter gourds to the pan and mix well. Sprinkle over the gram flour. Cover and simmer over a low heat for 5–8 minutes or until all of the gram flour has been absorbed into the sauce. Serve garnished with fresh coriander sprigs.

NUTRITIONAL NOTES	
Per Portion	
Energy	120Kcals/490KJ
Fat	3.50g
Saturated Fat	0.41g
Carbohydrate	9.20g
Fibre	0.40g

_____ COOK'S TIP _____

Bitter gourds, which are also known as karelas, resemble small cucumbers with a warty skin. True to their name, they are extremely bitter. The medium-sized ones (about 10cm/4in long) are usually slightly less bitter than the tiny ones.

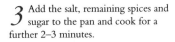

Balti Mushrooms in a Creamy Garlic Sauce

This is a simple and delicious Balti recipe which could be accompanied by one of the rice dishes from this book.

INGREDIENTS

Serves 4

350g/12oz/4½ cups button (white) mushrooms
15ml/1 tbsp oil
1 bay leaf
3 garlic cloves, roughly chopped
2 green chillies, seeded and chopped
225g/8oz/1 cup low fat fromage frais or crème fraîche
15ml/1 tbsp chopped fresh mint
15ml/1 tbsp chopped fresh coriander (cilantro)
5ml/1 tsp salt
fresh mint and coriander (cilantro) leaves, to garnish

1 Cut the mushrooms in half, or in quarters if large, and set aside.

<table>
<tr><td colspan="2" align="center">NUTRITIONAL NOTES
Per Portion</td></tr>
<tr><td>Energy</td><td>76Kcals/321KJ</td></tr>
<tr><td>Fat</td><td>3.40g</td></tr>
<tr><td>Saturated Fat</td><td>0.55g</td></tr>
<tr><td>Carbohydrate</td><td>5.20g</td></tr>
<tr><td>Fibre</td><td>1.10g</td></tr>
</table>

2 Heat the oil in a wok or heavy frying pan, then add the bay leaf, garlic and chillies and quickly stir-fry for about 1 minute.

3 Add the mushrooms. Stir-fry for another 2 minutes.

4 Remove from the heat and stir in the fromage frais or crème fraîche followed by the mint, coriander and salt. Return to the heat and stir-fry for 2–3 minutes, then transfer to a warmed serving dish and garnish with mint and coriander leaves.

--- COOK'S TIP ---

Cook the mushrooms for a few minutes longer if you like them to be well cooked and browned.

Balti Corn with Cauliflower

This quick and tasty vegetable side dish is most easily made with frozen corn.

INGREDIENTS

Serves 4
15ml/1 tbsp oil
4 curry leaves
1.5ml/¼ tsp onion seeds
2 medium onions, diced
1 red chilli, seeded and diced
175g/6oz/1 cup frozen corn
½ small cauliflower, cut
    into florets
3–7 mint leaves

NUTRITIONAL NOTES	
Per Portion	
Energy	124Kcals/519KJ
Fat	3.89g
Saturated Fat	0.58g
Carbohydrate	19.31g
Fibre	2.56g

—————— COOK'S TIP ——————

It is best to cook this dish immediately before serving and eating, as the flavour tends to spoil if it is kept warm.

1 Heat the oil in a wok or heavy frying pan and stir-fry the curry leaves and the onion seeds for about 30 seconds.

3 Add the red chilli, frozen corn and cauliflower florets and stir-fry for 5–8 minutes.

2 Add the onions and fry them for 5–8 minutes until golden brown.

4 Finally, add the mint leaves and serve immediately.

Courgettes with Mushrooms in a Yogurt Sauce

Yogurt makes a creamy sauce which is low in fat when served with mushrooms and courgettes.

Ingredients

Serves 4

15ml/1 tbsp oil
1 medium onion, roughly chopped
5ml/1 tsp ground coriander
5ml/1 tsp ground cumin
5ml/1 tsp salt
2.5ml/½ tsp chilli powder
225g/8oz/3 cups mushrooms, sliced
2 medium courgettes (zucchini), sliced
45ml/3 tbsp natural (plain) low fat yogurt
15ml/1 tbsp chopped fresh coriander
  (cilantro), to garnish (optional)

1 Heat the oil in a heavy pan and fry the onion until golden brown. Lower the heat to medium, add the ground coriander, cumin, salt and chilli powder and stir together well.

2 Once the onion and the spices are well blended, add the mushrooms and courgettes and stir-fry gently for about 5 minutes until soft. If the mixture is too dry, just add a little water to loosen.

3 Finally add the yogurt and mix it well into the vegetables.

4 Garnish with chopped fresh coriander, if wished, and serve immediately.

Nutritional Notes
Per Portion

Energy	64Kcals/265KJ
Fat	3.70g
Saturated Fat	0.58g
Carbohydrate	4.80g
Fibre	1.40g

Cook's Tip

Yogurt has a great affinity with stir-fried vegetables and this lovely combination of sliced courgettes (zucchini) and mushrooms would make a tasty accompaniment to serve with poultry or lamb dishes. If preferred, you could use aubergines (egg-plants) or mushrooms instead of courgettes.

Potatoes in Tomato Sauce

This curry makes an excellent accompaniment to almost any other dish, but goes particularly well with Balti dishes. Served with rice, it makes a great vegetarian main course.

INGREDIENTS

Serves 4
10ml/2 tsp oil
1.5ml/¼ tsp onion seeds
4 curry leaves
2 medium onions, diced
400g/14oz can tomatoes
5ml/1 tsp ground cumin
7.5ml/1½ tsp ground coriander
5ml/1 tsp chilli powder
5ml/1 tsp crushed fresh root ginger
5ml/1 tsp crushed garlic
1.5ml/¼ tsp ground turmeric
5ml/1 tsp salt
15ml/1 tbsp lemon juice
15ml/1 tbsp chopped fresh coriander
   (cilantro)
2 medium potatoes, diced

1 Heat the oil in a wok or heavy frying pan and fry the onion seeds, curry leaves and onions over medium heat for a few minutes, being careful not to burn the onions.

2 Meanwhile, place the canned tomatoes in a bowl and add the cumin, ground coriander, chilli powder, ginger, garlic, turmeric, salt, lemon juice and fresh coriander. Mix together until well blended.

_____ COOK'S TIP _____

This curry is also delicious if you add a few cauliflower or broccoli florets with the potatoes, or if you substitute diced parsnips for the potatoes.

3 Pour this mixture into the wok and stir for about 1 minute to mix thoroughly with the onions.

4 Finally, add the diced potatoes, cover the pan and cook gently for 7–10 minutes over low heat. Check that the potatoes are properly cooked through, then serve.

NUTRITIONAL NOTES *Per Portion*	
Energy	119Kcals/502KJ
Fat	2.27g
Saturated Fat	0.24g
Carbohydrate	22.91g
Fibre	2.88g

Green Beans with Corn

Frozen green beans are useful for this dish, as they are quick to cook. It makes an excellent vegetable accompaniment.

INGREDIENTS

Serves 4

15ml/1 tbsp oil
1.5ml/¼ tsp mustard seeds
1 medium red onion, diced
50g/2oz/⅓ cup frozen corn
50g/2oz/¼ cup canned red kidney beans, drained
175g/6oz frozen green beans
1 medium red chilli, seeded and diced
1 garlic clove, chopped
2.5cm/1in piece root ginger, finely chopped
15ml/1 tbsp chopped fresh coriander (cilantro)
5ml/1 tsp salt
1 medium tomato, seeded and diced, to garnish

1 Heat the oil in a wok or heavy frying pan for about 30 seconds, then add the mustard seeds and onion. Sti-fry for 2–3 minutes.

NUTRITIONAL NOTES	
Per Portion	
Energy	84Kcals/349KJ
Fat	3.44g
Saturated Fat	0.50g
Carbohydrate	11.13g
Fibre	2.70g

2 Add the corn, red kidney beans and green beans. Stir-fry for 3–5 minutes.

3 Add the chilli, chopped garlic and ginger, coriander and salt and stir-fry for 2–3 minutes.

4 Remove the pan from the heat. Transfer the vegetables to a serving dish and garnish with the diced tomato.

——— COOK'S TIP ———

This is a good stand-by dish as it uses frozen and canned ingredients. To make sure you have always got a chilli available for making it, freeze whole fresh chillies, unblanched, for use as required.

Potatoes with Red Chillies

The quantity of red chillies used here may be too fiery for some palates. For a milder version, seed the chillies, use fewer, or substitute them with a roughly chopped red pepper.

INGREDIENTS

Serves 4

12-14 baby new potatoes, peeled
  and halved
2.5ml/½ tsp salt
15ml/1 tbsp oil
2.5ml/½ tsp crushed dried red chillies
2.5ml/½ tsp cumin seeds
2.5ml/½ tsp fennel seeds
2.5ml/½ tsp crushed coriander seeds
1 medium onion, sliced
1–4 fresh red chillies, chopped
15ml/1 tbsp chopped fresh coriander
  (cilantro)

1 Boil the potatoes in salted water until soft but still firm. Remove from the heat and drain off the water.

NUTRITIONAL NOTES	
Per Portion	
Energy	122Kcals/513KJ
Fat	3.50g
Saturated Fat	0.37g
Carbohydrate	21.20g
Fibre	1.50g

2 In a deep heavy frying pan, heat the oil quickly over high heat, then turn down the heat to medium. Add the crushed chillies, cumin, fennel and coriander seeds and a little salt and quickly stir-fry for about 30–40 seconds.

3 Add the onion and fry gently until golden brown. Then add the new potatoes, fresh red chillies and fresh coriander.

4 Cover and cook for 5–7 minutes over a very low heat. Serve hot.

Sweet-and-sour Vegetables with Panir

The cheese used in this recipe is Indian panir, which can be bought at some Asian stores; tofu can be used in its place.

INGREDIENTS

Serves 4

1 green (bell) pepper, seeded and cut into squares
1 yellow (bell) pepper, seeded and cut into squares
8 cherry tomatoes
8 cauliflower florets
8 pineapple chunks
8 cubes panir
plain, boiled rice, to serve

For the seasoned oil

15ml/1 tbsp oil
30ml/2 tbsp lemon juice
5ml/1 tsp salt
5ml/1 tsp crushed black peppercorns
15ml/1 tbsp clear honey
30ml/2 tbsp chilli sauce

NUTRITIONAL NOTES	
Per Portion	
Energy	75Kcals/311KJ
Fat	3.30g
Saturated Fat	0.38g
Carbohydrate	9.90g
Fibre	2.10g

1 Preheat the grill (broiler) to hot. Thread the green and yellow pepper squares, cherry tomatoes, cauliflower florets, pineapple chunks and panir cubes on to four skewers, alternating the ingredients. Arrange the skewers on a flameproof dish or in a grill pan.

2 In a small bowl, mix all the ingredients for the seasoned oil. If too thick, add 15ml/1 tbsp water.

--- COOK'S TIP ---

To make panir at home, bring 1 litre/ 1¾ pints/4 cups milk to boil over a low heat. Add 30ml/2 tbsp lemon juice and stir until it thickens and begins to curdle. Strain through a sieve lined with muslin (cheesecloth). Set aside under a heavy weight for 1 hour until about 1cm/½in thick. Use the next day when it will be firmer to handle.

3 Brush the vegetables with the seasoned oil. Grill (broil) for about 10 minutes until the vegetables begin to darken slightly, turning the skewers to cook evenly. Serve on a bed of plain boiled rice.

Vegetables and Beans with Curry Leaves

Bright, shiny green curry leaves look like small bay leaves, though not as tough. They are a popular seasoning ingredient in Indian cooking, adding a spicy flavour to dishes such as this dry curry.

INGREDIENTS

Serves 4

15ml/1 tbsp oil
6 curry leaves
3 garlic cloves, sliced
3 dried red chillies
1.5ml/¼ tsp onion seeds
1.5ml/¼ tsp fenugreek seeds
3 fresh green chillies, chopped
115g/4oz/½ cup canned red kidney
   beans, drained
1 medium carrot, cut into strips
50g/2oz green beans, sliced diagonally
1 medium red (bell) pepper, seeded and
   cut into strips
5ml/1 tsp salt
30ml/2 tbsp lemon juice

NUTRITIONAL NOTES	
Per Portion	
Energy	79Kcals/331KJ
Fat	3.30g
Saturated Fat	0.37g
Carbohydrate	9.70g
Fibre	2.60g

————— COOK'S TIP —————

Fresh curry leaves are very aromatic and there is no substitute. It is worth freezing fresh ones so you always have a supply.

1 Heat the oil in a deep heavy frying pan. Add the curry leaves, garlic cloves, dried chillies, and onion and fenugreek seeds.

2 When these ingredients turn a shade darker, add the chillies, kidney beans, carrot strips, green beans and pepper strips, stirring constantly. Stir in the salt and the lemon juice. Lower the heat, cover and cook for about 5 minutes.

3 Transfer the hot curry to a serving dish and serve immediately.

Corn and Pea Curry

Tender corn is cooked in a spicy tomato sauce.

Ingredients

Serves 4

6 pieces of frozen corn on the
   cob, thawed
15ml/1 tbsp oil
2.5ml/½ tsp cumin seeds
1 onion, finely chopped
2 garlic cloves, crushed
1 green chilli, finely chopped
15ml/1 tbsp curry paste
5ml/1 tsp ground coriander
5ml/1 tsp ground cumin
1.5ml/¼ tsp ground turmeric
2.5ml/½ tsp salt
2.5ml/½ tsp sugar
400g/14oz can chopped tomatoes
15ml/1 tbsp tomato purée (paste)
150ml/¼ pint/⅔ cup water
115g/4oz/1 cup frozen peas, thawed
30ml/2 tbsp chopped fresh coriander
   (cilantro)
chappatis, to serve (optional)

Nutritional Notes	
Per Portion	
Energy	159Kcals/669KJ
Fat	5.20g
Saturated Fat	0.48g
Carbohydrate	23.00g
Fibre	4.60g

1 Using a sharp knife, cut each piece of corn in half crossways to make 12 equal pieces in total.

2 Bring a large pan of water to the boil and cook the corn cob pieces for 10–12 minutes. Drain well.

3 Heat the oil in a large heavy pan and fry the cumin seeds for 2 minutes or until they begin to splutter. Add the onion, garlic and chilli and fry for about 5–6 minutes until the onion is golden.

4 Add the curry paste and fry for 2 minutes. Stir in the remaining spices, salt and sugar and fry for a further 2–3 minutes, adding some water if the mixture is too dry.

5 Add the chopped tomatoes and tomato purée together with the water and simmer for 5 minutes or until the sauce thickens. Add the peas and cook for a further 5 minutes.

6 Add the pieces of corn and fresh coriander and cook for a further 6–8 minutes or until the corn and peas are tender. Serve with chappatis, for mopping up the rich sauce, if you like.

Cook's Tip

If you don't like peas you can replace them with the same quantity of frozen or canned corn if wished.

Vegetables with Almonds

Low fat natural yogurt is added to the vegetables towards the end of the cooking time, which not only gives this dish a tangy flavour but also makes it creamy.

INGREDIENTS

Serves 4

30ml/2 tbsp oil
2 medium onions, sliced
5cm/2in piece root ginger, shredded
5ml/1 tsp crushed black peppercorns
1 bay leaf
1.5ml/¼ tsp ground turmeric
5ml/1 tsp ground coriander
5ml/1 tsp salt
2.5ml/½ tsp garam masala
175g/6oz/2½ cups mushrooms, sliced
1 medium courgette (zucchini), thickly
    sliced
50g/2oz green beans, cut into
    2.5cm/1in lengths
15ml/1 tbsp roughly chopped fresh mint
150ml/¼ pint/⅔ cup water
30ml/2 tbsp natural (plain) low fat yogurt
25g/1oz/¼ cup flaked (sliced) almonds

1 In a heavy deep frying pan, heat the oil and fry the onions with the ginger, peppercorns and bay leaf for 3–5 minutes.

NUTRITIONAL NOTES	
Per Portion	
Energy	140Kcals/579KJ
Fat	9.80g
Saturated Fat	1.13g
Carbohydrate	9.00g
Fibre	2.20g

2 Lower the heat and add the turmeric, ground coriander, salt and garam masala, stirring occasionally. Gradually add the sliced mushrooms, courgette, green beans and mint. Stir gently to coat the vegetables, being careful not to break them up.

3 Pour in the water and bring to a simmer, then lower the heat and cook until the water has been totally absorbed by the vegetables.

4 Beat the yogurt lightly with a fork, then pour it on to the vegetables in the pan and mix together well until the vegetables are coated.

5 Cook the vegetables for a further 2–3 minutes, stirring occasionally. Serve immediately, garnished with the flaked almonds.

Carrot and Cauliflower Stir-fry

The carrots are thinly sliced into thin batons, which means that they cook quickly. This dish has a crunchy texture and only a few whole spices.

INGREDIENTS

Serves 4
2 large carrots
1 small cauliflower
15ml/1 tbsp oil
1 bay leaf
2 cloves
1 small cinnamon stick
2 cardamom pods
3 black peppercorns
5ml/1 tsp salt
50g/2oz/½ cup frozen peas, thawed
10ml/2 tsp lemon juice
15ml/1 tbsp chopped fresh coriander (cilantro), plus extra leaves, to garnish

1 Cut the carrots into thin batons about 2.5cm/1in long. Separate the cauliflower into small florets.

NUTRITIONAL NOTES	
Per Portion	
Energy	84Kcals/349KJ
Fat	3.75g
Saturated Fat	0.60g
Carbohydrate	9.05g
Fibre	3.67g

2 Heat the oil in a wok or heavy frying pan and add the bay leaf, cloves, cinnamon stick, cardamom pods and peppercorns. Quickly stir-fry over medium heat for 30–35 seconds, then add the salt.

3 Next add the carrot batons and cauliflower florets and continue to stir-fry for 3–5 minutes.

4 Add the peas, lemon juice and chopped coriander and cook for a further 4–5 minutes. Serve garnished with the whole coriander leaves.

_____ COOK'S TIP _____

As both carrots and cauliflower can be eaten raw, they need only minimal cooking or they will lose their crunchy texture.

Masala Mashed Potatoes

INGREDIENTS

Serves 4

3 medium potatoes
15ml/1 tbsp chopped fresh mint and
    coriander (cilantro), mixed
5ml/1 tsp mango powder
5ml/1 tsp salt
5ml/1 tsp crushed black peppercorns
1 red chilli, chopped
1 green chilli, chopped
50g/2oz/4 tbsp low fat margarine

1 Boil the potatoes until soft then
mash them down using a masher.

NUTRITIONAL NOTES	
Per Portion	
Energy	100Kcals/416KJ
Fat	5.30g
Saturated Fat	1.25g
Carbohydrate	11.40g
Fibre	0.80g

2 Blend together the remaining
ingredients in a small bowl.

3 Stir the spice mixture into the
mashed potatoes. Mix together
thoroughly with a fork and serve warm
as an accompaniment.

_____ COOK'S TIP _____

Mango powder, also known as *amchur*, is
the unripe green fruit of the mango tree
ground to a powder. The sour mangoes are
sliced and dried in the sun, turning a light
brown, before they are ground. Mango
powder adds a fruity sharpness, and a
slightly resinous bouquet, to a dish. It is
widely used with vegetables and is usually
added towards the end of the cooking time.
If mango powder is unavailable, the nearest
substitute is lemon or lime juice, in double
or treble quantity.

Spicy Cabbage

INGREDIENTS

Serves 4

50g/2oz/4 tbsp low fat margarine
2.5ml/½ tsp white cumin seeds
3-8 dried red chillies, to taste
1 small onion, sliced
225g/8oz/2½ cups cabbage, shredded
2 medium carrots, grated
2.5ml/½ tsp salt
30ml/2 tbsp lemon juice

NUTRITIONAL NOTES	
Per Portion	
Energy	91Kcals/376KJ
Fat	5.50g
Saturated Fat	1.27g
Carbohydrate	8.50g
Fibre	2.40g

1 Melt the margarine in a medium
pan and fry the cumin seeds and
dried chillies for about 30 seconds.

2 Add the onion and fry for about
2 minutes. Add the cabbage and
carrots and stir-fry for a further
5 minutes or until the cabbage is soft.

3 Finally, stir in the salt and lemon
juice and serve at once.

Balti Potatoes with Aubergines

Using baby potatoes adds to the attractiveness of this dish. Choose the smaller variety of aubergines, too, as they are far tastier than the large ones, which contain a lot of water and little flavour. Small aubergines are readily available from specialist grocers.

Ingredients

Serves 4

10–12 baby potatoes
6 small aubergines (eggplants)
1 medium red (bell) pepper
15ml/1 tbsp oil
2 medium onions, sliced
4–6 curry leaves
2.5ml/½ tsp onion seeds
5ml/1 tsp crushed coriander seeds
2.5ml/½ tsp cumin seeds
5ml/1 tsp crushed fresh root ginger
5ml/1 tsp crushed garlic
5ml/1 tsp crushed dried red chillies
15ml/1 tbsp chopped fresh fenugreek
5ml/1 tsp chopped fresh coriander
    (cilantro), plus extra to garnish
15ml/1 tbsp natural (plain) low fat yogurt

1 Cook the unpeeled potatoes in a pan of boiling water until they are just soft, but not broken down. Set them aside.

_____ Cook's Tip _____

Remember to whisk yogurt before adding it to a hot dish to prevent it from curdling.

2 Cut the aubergines into quarters, or eighths if using large aubergines.

3 Cut the pepper in half, remove the seeds and ribs, then slice the flesh into thin even-sized strips.

4 Heat the oil in a wok or heavy frying pan and fry the sliced onions, curry leaves, onion seeds, crushed coriander seeds and cumin seeds until the onion slices are a soft golden brown, stirring constantly.

5 Add the ginger, garlic, crushed chillies and fenugreek, followed by the aubergines and potatoes. Stir everything together and cover the wok with a lid. Lower the heat and cook the vegetables for 5–7 minutes.

6 Remove the lid, add the fresh coriander followed by the yogurt and stir well. Serve garnished with coriander leaves.

Nutritional Notes	
Per Portion	
Energy	183Kcals/773KJ
Fat	4.42g
Saturated Fat	0.70g
Carbohydrate	33.02g
Fibre	5.43g

Spiced Potatoes and Tomatoes

Diced potatoes are cooked gently in a fresh tomato sauce, which is flavoured with curry leaves and green chillies.

INGREDIENTS

Serves 4

2 medium potatoes
15ml/1 tbsp oil
2 medium onions, finely chopped
4 curry leaves
1.5ml/¼ tsp onion seeds
1 green chilli, seeded and chopped
4 tomatoes, sliced
5ml/1 tsp crushed fresh root ginger
5ml/1 tsp crushed garlic
5ml/1 tsp chilli powder
5ml/1 tsp ground coriander
1.5ml/¼ tsp salt
5ml/1 tsp lemon juice
15ml/1 tbsp chopped fresh coriander
   (cilantro)
3 hard-boiled eggs, to garnish

1 Peel the potatoes and cut them into small cubes.

NUTRITIONAL NOTES	
Per Portion	
Energy	188Kcals/790KJ
Fat	7.62g
Saturated Fat	1.66g
Carbohydrate	23.41g
Fibre	3.10g

2 Heat the oil in a wok or heavy frying pan and stir-fry the onions, curry leaves, onion seeds and green chilli for about 40 seconds.

3 Add the tomatoes and cook for about 2 minutes over low heat.

4 Add the ginger and garlic, chilli powder, ground coriander and salt to taste. Continue to stir-fry for 1–2 minutes, then add the potatoes and cook over a low heat for 5–7 minutes until the potatoes are tender.

5 Add the lemon juice and fresh coriander and stir to mix together.

6 Shell the hard-boiled eggs, cut into quarters, and add as a garnish to the finished dish.

_____ COOK'S TIP _____

Drain the hard-boiled eggs and cool them under cold running water, then tap the shells and leave the eggs until cold. This prevents a discoloured rim forming round the outside of the yolk and enables the shell to be removed easily.

Baked Potato with Spicy Cottage Cheese

Always choose a variety of potato recommended for baking for this recipe, as the texture of the potato should not be too dry. This makes an excellent low fat snack at any time of the day.

Ingredients

Serves 4
4 medium baking potatoes
225g/8oz/1 cup low fat cottage cheese
10ml/2 tsp tomato purée (paste)
2.5ml/½ tsp ground cumin
2.5ml/½ tsp ground coriander
2.5ml/½ tsp chilli powder
2.5ml/½ tsp salt
15ml/1 tbsp oil
2.5ml/½ tsp mixed onion and
    mustard seeds
3 curry leaves
30ml/2 tbsp water

For the garnish
mixed salad leaves
fresh coriander (cilantro) sprigs
lemon wedges
2 tomatoes, quartered

1 Preheat the oven to 180°C/350°F/ Gas 4. Wash, pat dry and make a slit in the middle of each potato. Prick the potatoes a few times with a fork or skewer, then wrap them individually in foil. Bake in the oven directly on the shelf for about 1 hour, or until soft.

2 Put the cottage cheese into a heatproof dish and set aside.

3 In a separate bowl, mix well together the tomato purée, ground cumin, ground coriander, chilli powder and salt.

4 Heat the oil in a small pan for about 1 minute. Add the mixed onion and mustard seeds and the curry leaves and tilt the pan so the oil covers all the seeds and leaves.

--- Cook's Tip ---

This recipe can also be used as a basis for a tangy vegetable accompaniment to a main meal. Instead of using baked potatoes, boil some small new potatoes in their skins, then cut each one in half. Add the cooked potatoes to the spicy cottage cheese mixture, mix together well and serve.

5 When the curry leaves turn a shade darker and you can smell their beautiful aroma, pour the tomato purée mixture into the pan and turn the heat immediately to low. Add the water and mix well. Cook for a further minute, then pour the spicy tomato mixture on to the cottage cheese and stir together well.

6 Check that the baked potatoes are cooked right through, by inserting a knife or skewer into the middle of the flesh. If it is soft, unwrap the potatoes from the foil and divide the cottage cheese equally between them.

7 Garnish the filled potatoes with mixed salad leaves, fresh coriander sprigs, lemon wedges and tomato quarters and serve hot.

Nutritional Notes	
Per Portion	
Energy	175Kcals/740KJ
Fat	4.30g
Saturated Fat	0.43g
Carbohydrate	24.40g
Fibre	1.90g

Potatoes in a Yogurt Sauce

It is nice to use tiny new potatoes with the skins on for this recipe. The yogurt adds a tangy flavour to this fairly spicy dish, which is delicious served with plain or wholemeal chappatis.

INGREDIENTS

Serves 4

12 new potatoes, halved
275g/10oz/1¼ cups natural (plain)
   low fat yogurt
300ml/½ pint/1¼ cups water
1.5ml/¼ tsp ground turmeric
5ml/1 tsp chilli powder
5ml/1 tsp ground coriander
2.5ml/½ tsp ground cumin
5ml/1 tsp soft brown sugar
1.5ml/¼ tsp salt
15ml/1 tbsp oil
5ml/1 tsp cumin seeds
15ml/1 tbsp chopped fresh coriander
   (cilantro)
2 green chillies, sliced

--- COOK'S TIP ---

If new potatoes are unavailable, use 450g/1lb ordinary potatoes instead. Peel them and cut into large chunks, then cook as described above.

1 Boil the potatoes in salted water with their skins on until they are just tender, then drain and set aside.

2 Mix together the yogurt, water, turmeric, chilli powder, ground coriander, ground cumin, sugar and salt in a bowl. Set aside.

3 Heat the oil in a medium heavy pan and stir in the cumin seeds. Fry for 1 minute.

4 Reduce the heat, stir in the spicy yogurt mixture and cook for about 3 minutes over medium heat.

5 Add the chopped fresh coriander, green chillies and cooked potatoes. Blend everything together and cook for a further 5–7 minutes, stirring from time to time. Serve hot.

NUTRITIONAL NOTES	
Per Portion	
Energy	169Kcals/712KJ
Fat	4.30g
Saturated Fat	0.78g
Carbohydrate	27.60g
Fibre	1.20g

Okra with Green Mango and Lentils

If you like okra, you'll love this
spicy tangy dish.

INGREDIENTS

Serves 4

115g/4oz/½ cup *toor dhal*
15ml/1 tbsp oil
2.5ml/½ tsp onion seeds
2 onions, sliced
2.5ml/½ tsp ground fenugreek
1.5ml/¼ tsp ground turmeric
5ml/1 tsp ground coriander
7.5ml/1½ tsp chilli powder
5ml/1 tsp crushed fresh root ginger
5ml/1 tsp crushed garlic
1 green mango, peeled and sliced
450g/1lb okra, trimmed and cut
    into 1cm/½in pieces
7.5ml/1½ tsp salt
2 red chillies, seeded and sliced
30ml/2 tbsp chopped fresh
    coriander (cilantro)
1 tomato, sliced

1 Wash the *toor dhal* thoroughly to
remove any grit and place in a
large pan with enough cold water to
cover. Bring to the boil and cook
until soft but not mushy. Drain and set
to one side while cooking the mango
and okra.

2 Heat the oil in a heavy round-
bottomed frying pan and fry the
onion seeds until they begin to pop.
Add the onions and fry until golden
brown. Lower the heat and add the
ground fenugreek, turmeric and
coriander, the chilli powder and the
crushed ginger and garlic.

3 Add the mango slices and the okra
pieces. Stir well and then add the
salt, red chillies and fresh coriander.
Stir-fry for 3–4 minutes or until the
okra is well cooked and tender.

4 Finally, add the cooked dhal and
sliced tomato and cook for a
further 3 minutes. Serve hot.

_____ COOK'S TIP _____

When buying okra, always choose small,
bright green ones with no brown patches.
Trim off the conical cap, taking care not to
pierce through to the seed pod where there
are tiny edible seeds and a sticky juice.

NUTRITIONAL NOTES
Per Portion

Energy	229Kcals/963KJ
Fat	5.00g
Saturated Fat	0.55g
Carbohydrate	36.00g
Fibre	8.10g

Balti Potatoes

The potato is transformed into something quite exotic when it is cooked like this with a delicious mixture of spices.

INGREDIENTS

Serves 4

15ml/1 tbsp oil
5ml/1 tsp cumin seeds
3 curry leaves
5ml/1 tsp crushed dried red chillies
2.5ml/½ tsp mixed onion, mustard and fenugreek seeds
2.5ml/½ tsp fennel seeds
3 garlic cloves, sliced
2.5cm/1in piece root ginger, grated
2 onions, sliced
6 new potatoes, thinly sliced
15ml/1 tbsp chopped fresh coriander (cilantro)
1 fresh red chilli, seeded and sliced
1 fresh green chilli, seeded and sliced

—————— COOK'S TIP ——————

Choose a waxy variety of new potato for this fairly hot vegetable dish; if you use a very soft potato, it will not cut into thin slices without breaking up. Leave the peel on for a tastier result.

	NUTRITIONAL NOTES
	Per Portion
Energy	110Kcals/462KJ
Fat	3.60g
Saturated Fat	0.39g
Carbohydrate	17.1g
Fibre	1.60g

1 Heat the oil in a heavy round-bottomed frying pan or wok. Lower the heat slightly and add the cumin seeds, curry leaves, dried red chillies, mixed onion, mustard and fenugreek seeds, fennel seeds, garlic cloves and ginger. Fry for 1 minute.

2 Add the onions and fry for a further 5 minutes, or until the onions are golden brown.

3 Add the potatoes, fresh coriander and fresh red and green chillies and mix well. Cover the pan tightly with a lid or foil; if using foil, make sure that it does not touch the food. Cook over a very low heat for about 7 minutes or until the potatoes are tender.

4 Remove the pan from the heat, take off the lid and serve hot.

RICE AND PULSE DISHES

No Indian meal is complete without a bread or rice accompaniment. Plain boiled basmati rice is the most popular way to serve rice, but try Tomato Rice or Pea and Mushroom Pilau for special occasions. Dhals are another popular side dish, particularly if served with curries that are rather dry in texture.

Chicken Biryani

Biryanis originated in Persia and are traditionally made with a combination of meat and rice. They are often served at dinner parties and on festive occasions.

INGREDIENTS

Serves 4

275g/10oz/1½ cups basmati rice
30ml/2 tbsp oil
1 onion, thinly sliced
2 garlic cloves, crushed
1 green chilli, finely chopped
2.5cm/1in piece root ginger, finely chopped
675g/1½lb chicken breast fillets, skinned and cut into 2.5cm/1in cubes
45ml/3 tbsp curry paste
1.5ml/¼ tsp salt
1.5ml/¼ tsp garam masala
3 tomatoes, cut into thin wedges
1.5ml/¼ tsp ground turmeric
2 bay leaves
4 green cardamom pods
4 cloves
1.5ml/¼ tsp saffron strands
Tomato and Chilli Chutney, to serve

1 Wash the rice in several changes of cold water. Put into a large bowl, cover with plenty of water and leave to soak for 30 minutes.

2 Meanwhile, heat the oil in a large heavy frying pan and fry the onion for about 5–7 minutes until lightly browned. Add the garlic, chilli and ginger and fry for about 2 minutes.

3 Add the chicken and fry for about 5 minutes, stirring occasionally.

4 Add the curry paste, salt and garam masala to the chicken mixture and cook for 5 minutes. Gently stir in the tomato wedges and continue cooking for another 3–4 minutes, then remove from the heat and set aside.

5 Preheat the oven to 190°C/375°F/ Gas 5. Bring a large pan of water to the boil. Drain the rice and add it to the pan with the turmeric. Cook for about 10 minutes, or until the rice is almost tender. Drain the rice and toss together with the bay leaves, cardamoms, cloves and saffron.

6 Layer the rice and chicken in a shallow, ovenproof dish until all the mixture has been used, finishing off with a layer of rice. Cover and bake in the oven for 15–20 minutes or until the chicken is tender. Serve with Tomato and Chilli Chutney.

NUTRITIONAL NOTES	
Per Portion	
Energy	531Kcals/2224KJ
Fat	14.10g
Saturated Fat	2.77g
Carbohydrate	61.30g
Fibre	3.70g

Vegetable Biryani

This exotic dish made from everyday ingredients will be appreciated by vegetarians and meat-eaters alike. It is extremely low in fat, but packed full of exciting flavours.

INGREDIENTS

Serves 4–6

175g/6oz/scant 1 cup long-grain rice
2 whole cloves
2 cardamom pods, seeds only
450ml/¾ pint/1¾ cups vegetable stock
2 garlic cloves
1 small onion, roughly chopped
5ml/1 tsp cumin seeds
5ml/1 tsp ground coriander
2.5ml/½ tsp ground turmeric
2.5ml/½ tsp chilli powder
salt and black pepper
1 large potato, cut into 2.5cm/
   1in cubes
2 carrots, sliced
½ cauliflower, broken into florets
50g/2oz green beans, cut into
   2.5cm/1in lengths
30ml/2 tbsp chopped fresh coriander
   (cilantro), plus a sprig to garnish
30ml/2 tbsp lime juice

NUTRITIONAL NOTES	
Per Portion (6)	
Energy	260Kcals/1100KJ
Fat	1.90g
Saturated Fat	0.07g
Carbohydrate	55.80g
Fibre	3.20g

--- COOK'S TIP ---

Substitute other vegetables for the ones chosen here, if you like. Courgettes (zucchinis), broccoli, parsnip and sweet potatoes would all be excellent choices. And even adding some toasted almond slices will not make the fat content of this dish too high.

1 Wash the rice and put it with the cloves and cardamom seeds into a large heavy pan. Pour over the stock and bring to the boil.

2 Reduce the heat, cover and simmer for 20 minutes or until all the stock has been absorbed.

3 Meanwhile, put the garlic cloves, onion, cumin seeds, ground coriander, turmeric, chilli powder and seasoning into a blender or coffee grinder together with 30ml/ 2 tbsp water. Blend to a smooth paste.

4 Preheat the oven to 180°C/350°F/ Gas 4. Spoon the spicy paste into a flameproof casserole and cook over a low heat on top of the stove for 2 minutes, stirring occasionally.

5 Add the potato cubes, carrots, cauliflower, beans and 90ml/6 tbsp water. Cover and cook over low heat for 12 minutes, stirring occasionally. Add the chopped fresh coriander.

6 Remove the cloves from the rice. Spoon the rice over the vegetables. Sprinkle with the lime juice. Cover and cook in the oven for 25 minutes or until the vegetables are tender. Fluff up the rice with a fork before serving and garnish with a sprig of fresh coriander.

Rice with Mushrooms and Prawns

Although mushrooms are not a particularly popular vegetable in India, this dish is a perfect combination of flavours.

INGREDIENTS

Serves 4

150g/5oz/²⁄₃ cup basmati rice
15ml/1 tbsp oil
1 medium onion, chopped
4 black peppercorns
2.5cm/1in cinnamon stick
1 bay leaf
1.5ml/¼ tsp cumin seeds
2 cardamom pods
5ml/1 tsp crushed garlic
5ml/1 tsp crushed fresh root ginger
5ml/1 tsp garam masala
5ml/1 tsp chilli powder
7.5ml/1½ tsp salt
115g/4oz/1 cup frozen cooked peeled
  prawns (shrimp), thawed
115g/4oz/1½ cups mushrooms, cut
  into large pieces
30ml/2 tbsp chopped fresh coriander
  (cilantro)
120ml/4fl oz/½ cup natural (plain)
  low fat yogurt
15ml/1 tbsp lemon juice
50g/2oz/½ cup frozen peas
250ml/8fl oz/1 cup water
1 red chilli, seeded and sliced, to garnish

NUTRITIONAL NOTES	
Per Portion	
Energy	248Kcals/1050KJ
Fat	5.20g
Saturated Fat	0.99g
Carbohydrate	40.04g
Fibre	1.85g

—————— COOK'S TIP ——————

Basmati rice grows in the foothills of the Himalayas. The delicate, slender grains have a unique aroma and flavour. The rice cooks to light, separate, fluffy grains, making it perfect for dishes such as this.

1 Wash the rice well and leave to soak in water for 30 minutes.

2 Heat the oil in a wok or heavy frying pan and add the onion, peppercorns, cinnamon, bay leaf, cumin seeds, cardamom pods, garlic, ginger, garam masala, chilli powder and salt. Lower the heat and stir-fry for 2–3 minutes.

3 Add the prawns to the spice mixture and cook for 2 minutes, before adding the mushrooms.

4 Add the coriander and the yogurt, followed by the lemon juice and peas and cook for 2 more minutes.

5 Drain the rice and add it to the prawn mixture. Pour in the water, cover the pan and cook over medium heat for about 15 minutes, checking once that it has not stuck to the pan.

6 Remove the pan from the heat and leave to stand, still covered, for about 5 minutes. Transfer to a serving dish and serve garnished with the sliced red chilli.

Masala Prawns and Rice

INGREDIENTS

Serves 4–6

2 large onions, sliced and boiled
300ml/½ pint/1¼ cups natural (plain)
   low fat yogurt
30ml/2 tbsp tomato purée (paste)
60ml/4 tbsp green masala paste
30ml/2 tbsp lemon juice
5ml/1 tsp black cumin seeds
5cm/2in cinnamon stick
4 green cardamom pods
1.5ml/¼ tsp salt
450g/1lb uncooked king prawns
   (jumbo shrimp), peeled and deveined
225g/8oz/3 cups button (white)
   mushrooms
225g/8oz/2 cups frozen peas, thawed
450g/1lb/generous 2¼ cups
   basmati rice
300ml/½ pint/1¼ cups water
1 sachet saffron powder mixed with
   90ml/6 tbsp milk
15ml/1 tbsp oil

1 Mix the onions, yogurt, tomato
purée, green masala paste, lemon
juice, black cumin seeds, cinnamon
stick and cardamom pods together in
a large bowl and add salt to taste. Mix
the prawns, mushrooms and peas into
the marinade and leave to absorb the
spices for at least 2 hours.

2 Wash the rice well, cover with
boiling water and leave to soak
for 5 minutes, then drain.

3 Grease the base of a heavy pan and
add the prawns, vegetables and any
marinade juice. Cover with the drained
rice and smooth the surface gently until
you have an even layer.

4 Pour the water all over the surface
of the rice. Make random holes
through the rice with the handle of a
spoon and pour in the saffron milk.

5 Sprinkle the oil over the surface
of the rice and place a circular
piece of foil directly on top. Cover
and steam gently over a low heat for
45–50 minutes until the rice is cooked.
Gently toss the rice, prawns and
vegetables together and serve hot.

NUTRITIONAL NOTES	
Per Portion (6)	
Energy	724Kcals/3036KJ
Fat	9.80g
Saturated Fat	3.32g
Carbohydrate	121.50g
Fibre	4.70g

Basmati Rice with Potato

Rice is eaten at all meals in
Indian and Pakistani homes.
There are several ways of cooking
rice and mostly whole spices
are used. Always choose a good-
quality basmati rice.

INGREDIENTS

Serves 4

300g/11oz/1½ cups basmati rice
15ml/1 tbsp oil
1 small cinnamon stick
1 bay leaf
1.5ml/¼ tsp black cumin seeds
3 green cardamom pods
1 medium onion, sliced
5ml/1 tsp crushed fresh root ginger
5ml/1 tsp crushed garlic
1.5ml/¼ tsp ground turmeric
7.5ml/1½ tsp salt
1 large potato, roughly diced
475ml/16fl oz/2 cups water
15ml/1 tbsp chopped fresh coriander
   (cilantro)

1 Wash the rice well and leave it to
soak in water for 30 minutes.
Heat the oil in a heavy pan, add the
cinnamon, bay leaf, black cumin seeds,
cardamoms and onion and cook for
about 2 minutes.

COOK'S TIP

Serve the rice and potato mixture using a
slotted spoon and handle it gently to avoid
breaking the delicate grains of rice.

2 Add the ginger, garlic, turmeric, salt
and potato and cook for 1 minute.

3 Drain the rice and add to the
potato and spices in the pan.

4 Stir to mix, then pour in the
water followed by the coriander.
Cover the pan with a lid and cook for
15–20 minutes. Remove from the heat
and leave to stand, still covered, for
5–10 minutes before serving.

NUTRITIONAL NOTES	
Per Portion	
Energy	371Kcals/1572KJ
Fat	5.72g
Saturated Fat	1.03g
Carbohydrate	77.36g
Fibre	1.62g

Basmati Rice with Prawns and Vegetables

This is an excellent combination of prawns (shrimp) and vegetables which is lightly flavoured with whole spices. Using frozen mixed vegetables speeds up the preparation time. Serve with a cool and refreshing raita.

INGREDIENTS

Serves 4

300g/11oz/1½ cups basmati rice
15ml/1 tbsp oil
2 medium onions, sliced
3 green cardamom pods
2.5cm/1in cinnamon stick
4 black peppercorns
1 bay leaf
1.5ml/¼ tsp black cumin seeds
2.5cm/1in piece root ginger, grated
2 garlic cloves, roughly chopped
2 green chillies, seeded and chopped
30ml/2 tbsp chopped fresh coriander (cilantro)
30ml/2 tbsp lemon juice
115g/4oz/1 cup frozen vegetables (carrots, beans, corn and peas)
175–225g/6–8oz/1½–2 cups frozen cooked peeled prawns (shrimp), thawed
475ml/16fl oz/2 cups water

NUTRITIONAL NOTES	
Per Portion	
Energy	410Kcals/1737KJ
Fat	6.33g
Saturated Fat	1.13g
Carbohydrate	72.33g
Fibre	1.37g

_____ COOK'S TIP _____

This makes a very impressive dinner party dish and looks attractive decorated with large prawns (jumbo shrimp) in their shells.

1 Wash the rice well in cold water and leave it to soak in plenty of water in a bowl for 30 minutes.

2 Heat the oil in a heavy pan and fry the onions, cardamoms, cinnamon stick, peppercorns, bay leaf, black cumin seeds, ginger, garlic and chillies for about 3 minutes, stirring continuously.

3 Add half the fresh coriander, the lemon juice, mixed vegetables and prawns. Stir for a further 3 minutes.

4 Drain the rice and add it to the pan. Gently stir in the water and bring to the boil. Lower the heat, add the remaining fresh coriander and cook, covered with a lid, for 15–20 minutes or until all the liquid has been absorbed and the rice is cooked. Allow to stand, still covered, for 5–7 minutes before serving.

Basmati Rice with Peas and Curry Leaves

This is a very simple rice dish, but full of flavour.

INGREDIENTS

Serves 4

300g/11oz/1½ cups basmati rice
15ml/1 tbsp oil
6–8 curry leaves
1.5ml/¼ tsp mustard seeds
1.5ml/¼ tsp onion seeds
30ml/2 tbsp fresh fenugreek leaves
5ml/1 tsp crushed garlic
5ml/1 tsp crushed fresh root ginger
5ml/1 tsp salt
115g/4oz/1 cup frozen peas
475ml/16fl oz/2 cups water

--- COOK'S TIP ---

Curry leaves freeze very well, so it is worth keeping a stock in the freezer.

1 Wash the rice well and leave it to soak in water for 30 minutes.

NUTRITIONAL NOTES	
Per Portion	
Energy	336Kcals/1425KJ
Fat	5.96g
Saturated Fat	1.09g
Carbohydrate	67.67g
Fibre	1.83g

2 Heat the oil in a heavy pan with the curry leaves, mustard seeds, onion seeds, fenugreek, crushed garlic, crushed fresh root ginger and salt and stir-fry for 2–3 minutes.

3 Drain the rice, add it to the pan and stir gently.

4 Add the frozen peas and water and bring to the boil. Lower the heat, cover with a lid and cook for 15–20 minutes. Remove from the heat and leave to stand, still covered, for 10 minutes before serving.

Tomato Rice

Although generally served as an accompaniment to meat, poultry or fish dishes, this tasty rice dish can also be eaten as a complete meal on its own.

INGREDIENTS

Serves 4

400g/14oz/2 cups basmati rice
15ml/1 tbsp oil
2.5ml/½ tsp onion seeds
1 medium onion, sliced
2 medium tomatoes, sliced
1 orange or yellow (bell) pepper, seeded and sliced
5ml/1 tsp crushed fresh root ginger
5ml/1 tsp crushed garlic
5ml/1 tsp chilli powder
30ml/2 tbsp chopped fresh coriander (cilantro)
1 medium potato, diced
7.5ml/1½ tsp salt
50g/2oz/⅓ cup frozen peas
750ml/1¼ pints/3 cups water

1 Wash the rice well and leave it to soak in water for 30 minutes. Heat the oil in a heavy pan and fry the onion seeds for about 30 seconds. Add the sliced onion and fry for 5 minutes, stirring occasionally to prevent them sticking to the pan.

2 Add the sliced tomatoes and pepper, ginger, garlic, chilli powder, fresh coriander, potato, salt and peas and stir-fry over medium heat for a further 5 minutes.

3 Drain the rice, add to the pan and stir-fry for 1–2 minutes.

4 Pour in the water and bring to the boil, then lower the heat to medium. Cover and cook the rice for 12–15 minutes. Leave to stand for 5 minutes and then serve.

NUTRITIONAL NOTES *Per Portion*	
Energy	409Kcals/1710KJ
Fat	3.70g
Saturated Fat	0.44g
Carbohydrate	89.70g
Fibre	2.40g

_____ COOK'S TIP _____

Plain rice can look a bit dull; it is greatly enhanced by adding colourful ingredients such as tomatoes, (bell) peppers and peas.

Chicken Pilau

This chicken dish is a complete meal on its own, but is also delicious served with a lentil dish such as *Tarka Dhal*.

INGREDIENTS

Serves 4

400g/14oz/2 cups basmati rice
75g/3oz/6 tbsp low fat margarine
1 medium onion, sliced
1.5ml/¼ tsp mixed onion and mustard seeds
3 curry leaves
5ml/1 tsp crushed fresh root ginger
5ml/1 tsp crushed garlic
5ml/1 tsp ground coriander
5ml/1 tsp chilli powder
7.5ml/1½ tsp salt
2 tomatoes, sliced
1 medium potato, cubed
50g/2oz/⅓ cup frozen peas
175g/6oz chicken fillets, skinned and cubed
60ml/4 tbsp chopped fresh coriander (cilantro)
2 green chillies, chopped
750ml/1¼ pints/3 cups water

NUTRITIONAL NOTES	
Per Portion	
Energy	534Kcals/2231KJ
Fat	10.40g
Saturated Fat	2.48g
Carbohydrate	94.30g
Fibre	2.10g

--- COOK'S TIP ---

When you add the chicken cubes to the pan, stir them well to coat on all sides with the spice mixture; this will help to seal in the juices during cooking.

1 Wash the rice and soak in cold water for 30 minutes, then set aside in a sieve (strainer) to drain.

2 In a medium heavy pan, melt the low fat margarine and gently fry the onion until golden brown.

3 Add the mixed onion and mustard seeds, the curry leaves, ginger, garlic, ground coriander, chilli powder and salt. Stir-fry for about 2 minutes.

4 Add the tomatoes, potato, peas and chicken to the onion and mix everything together well.

5 Add the rice to the pan and stir gently to combine with all the other ingredients.

6 Finally, add the fresh coriander and green chillies. Mix and stir-fry for a further 1 minute. Pour in the water.

7 Bring the rice rapidly to the boil then lower the heat. Cover and cook for about 20 minutes. Transfer to a warmed dish and serve at once.

Vegetable Pilau

This vegetable rice dish goes well with most Indian meat dishes.

INGREDIENTS

Serves 4–6

225g/8oz/1 cup basmati rice
30ml/2 tbsp oil
2.5ml/½ tsp cumin seeds
2 bay leaves
4 green cardamom pods
4 cloves
1 onion, finely chopped
1 carrot, finely diced
50g/2oz/½ cup frozen peas, thawed
50g/2oz/⅓ cup frozen corn, thawed
25g/1oz/¼ cup cashew nuts,
  lightly fried
475ml/16fl oz/2 cups water
1.5ml/¼ tsp ground cumin
1.5ml/¼ tsp salt

1 Wash the basmati rice in several changes of cold water. Put into a bowl and cover with water. Leave to soak for 30 minutes.

NUTRITIONAL NOTES	
Per Portion (6)	
Energy	320Kcals/1334KJ
Fat	9.70g
Saturated Fat	1.14g
Carbohydrate	54.20g
Fibre	1.90g

2 Heat the oil in a large heavy frying pan and fry the cumin seeds for 2 minutes. Add the bay leaves, cardamom pods and cloves and fry for a further 2 minutes.

3 Add the onion and fry for 5 minutes until lightly browned.

4 Stir in the finely diced carrot and cook for 3–4 minutes.

5 Drain the rice and add to the pan with the peas, corn and cashew nuts. Fry for 4–5 minutes.

6 Add the water, ground cumin and salt. Bring to the boil, cover the pan and simmer for 15 minutes over a low heat until all the water is absorbed. Leave to stand, covered, for 10 minutes before serving.

COOK'S TIP

You can vary the vegetables and use any selection of your choice. If you want to use different fresh vegetables, courgettes (zucchini) cut into slices, or green beans would be equally good.

Pea and Mushroom Pilau

Mushrooms and peas make this delectable rice dish look truly attractive and appetizing.

INGREDIENTS

Serves 6
450g/1lb/2¼ cups basmati rice
15ml/1 tbsp oil
2.5ml/½ tsp cumin seeds
2 black cardamom pods
2 cinnamon sticks
3 garlic cloves, sliced
5ml/1 tsp salt
1 medium tomato, sliced
50g/2oz/²⁄₃ cup button (white) mushrooms
75g/3oz/generous ⅓ cup petits pois (baby peas)
750ml/1¼ pints/3 cups water

1 Wash the rice well and leave it to soak in water for 30 minutes.

2 In a medium heavy pan, heat the oil and add the spices, garlic and salt.

3 Add the tomato and mushrooms and stir-fry for 2–3 minutes.

4 Drain the rice and add it to the pan with the peas. Stir gently, making sure that you do not break up the grains of rice.

5 Add the water and bring to the boil. Lower the heat, cover and continue to cook for 15–20 minutes.

NUTRITIONAL NOTES	
Per Portion	
Energy	423Kcals/1768KJ
Fat	3.80g
Saturated Fat	0.39g
Carbohydrate	92.90g
Fibre	1.30g

_____ COOK'S TIP _____

Petits pois are small green peas, picked when very young. The tender, sweet peas inside are ideal for this delicately flavoured rice dish. However, if you can't find petit pois, garden peas can be used instead.

Indian Pilau Rice

INGREDIENTS

Serves 4

225g/8oz/1¼ cups basmati rice
15ml/1 tbsp oil
1 small onion, finely chopped
1 garlic clove, crushed
5ml/1 tsp fennel seeds
15ml/1 tbsp sesame seeds
2.5ml/½ tsp ground turmeric
5ml/1 tsp ground cumin
1.5ml/¼ tsp salt
2 whole cloves
4 cardamom pods, lightly crushed
5 black peppercorns
450ml/¾ pint/1¾ cups chicken stock
fresh coriander (cilantro), to garnish

NUTRITIONAL NOTES	
Per Portion	
Energy	265Kcals/1108KJ
Fat	6.00g
Saturated Fat	0.68g
Carbohydrate	49.50g
Fibre	0.60g

1 Wash the rice well and leave to soak in water for 30 minutes. Heat the oil in a heavy pan, add the onion and garlic and fry gently for 5–6 minutes until softened.

2 Stir in the fennel and sesame seeds, the turmeric, cumin, salt, cloves, cardamom pods and peppercorns and fry for about a minute. Drain the rice well, add to the pan and stir-fry for a further 3 minutes.

3 Pour on the chicken stock. Bring to the boil, then cover, reduce the heat to very low and simmer gently for 20 minutes, without removing the lid, until all the liquid has been absorbed.

_____ COOK'S TIP _____

In South India, where large quantities of rice are eaten, people prefer a rice which will absorb the spicy flavours of seasonings. In this recipe, basmati rice is cooked in the traditional way to seal in all the flavour.

4 Remove from the heat and leave to stand for 2–3 minutes. Fork up the rice, garnish with coriander and transfer to a warmed dish to serve.

Kidney Bean Curry

This is a popular Punjabi-style dish using red kidney beans. You can substitute the same quantity of other pulses, if you prefer.

INGREDIENTS

Serves 4

225g/8oz/1⅓ cups dried red
   kidney beans
30ml/2 tbsp oil
2.5ml/½ tsp cumin seeds
1 onion, thinly sliced
1 green chilli, finely chopped
2 garlic cloves, crushed
2.5cm/1in piece root ginger, grated
30ml/2 tbsp curry paste
5ml/1 tsp ground cumin
5ml/1 tsp ground coriander
2.5ml/½ tsp chilli powder
2.5ml/½ tsp salt
400g/14oz can chopped tomatoes
30ml/2 tbsp chopped coriander (cilantro)

1 Leave the kidney beans to soak overnight in a bowl of cold water.

2 Drain the beans and put in a large pan with double the volume of water. Boil vigorously for 10 minutes. Skim off any scum. Cover and cook for 1–1½ hours or until the beans are soft.

3 Meanwhile, heat the oil in a large heavy pan and fry the cumin seeds for 2 minutes until they begin to splutter. Add the onion, chilli, garlic and ginger and fry for 5 minutes. Stir in the curry paste, cumin, ground coriander, chilli powder and salt and cook for 5 minutes.

NUTRITIONAL NOTES
Per Portion

Energy	258Kcals/1087KJ
Fat	7.80g
Saturated Fat	0.86g
Carbohydrate	33.70g
Fibre	11.70g

4 Add the tomatoes and simmer for 5 minutes. Add the beans and fresh coriander, reserving a little for the garnish. Cover and cook for 15 minutes, adding a little water if necessary. Serve garnished with the reserved fresh coriander.

—— COOK'S TIP ——

If you want to reduce the cooking time, cook the beans in a pressure cooker for 20–25 minutes after boiling them vigorously for 10 minutes. Alternatively, replace the dried beans with canned beans. Use a 400g/14oz can and drain well before adding to the dish.

Tarka Dhal

Tarka Dhal is probably the most popular of Indian lentil dishes and is found today in most Indian/Pakistani restaurants.

INGREDIENTS

Serves 4
115g/4oz/¼ cup *masoor dhal*
50g/2oz/¼ cup *moong dhal*
600ml/1 pint/2½ cups water
5ml/1 tsp crushed fresh root ginger
5ml/1 tsp crushed garlic
1.5ml/¼ tsp ground turmeric
2 fresh green chillies, chopped
7.5ml/1½ tsp salt

For the *tarka*
30ml/2 tbsp oil
1 onion, sliced
1.5ml/¼ tsp mixed mustard and
  onion seeds
4 dried red chillies
1 tomato, sliced

For the garnish
15ml/1 tbsp chopped fresh coriander
  (cilantro)
1–2 green chillies, seeded and sliced
15ml/1 tbsp chopped fresh mint

1 Boil the two lentils in the water with the crushed ginger and garlic, turmeric and chopped green chillies for 15–20 minutes until soft.

2 Mash the lentil mixture with a fork or pound with a rolling pin until the consistency of a creamy chicken soup.

3 If the lentil mixture looks too dry, add a little more water. Season with the salt. To prepare the *tarka*, heat the oil in a heavy frying pan and fry the onion with the mustard and onion seeds, dried red chillies and tomato for 2 minutes.

NUTRITIONAL NOTES	
Per Portion	
Energy	162Kcals/681KJ
Fat	6.60g
Saturated Fat	0.74g
Carbohydrate	18.70g
Fibre	3.20g

4 Pour the *tarka* over the mashed lentils and garnish with fresh coriander, green chillies and mint.

_____ COOK'S TIP _____

Dried red chillies are available in many different sizes. If the ones you have are large, or if you want a less spicy flavour, reduce the quantity specified to 1–2.

Lentils and Rice

Lentils are cooked with whole and ground spices, potato, rice and onion to produce an authentic Indian-style risotto.

INGREDIENTS

Serves 4

150g/5oz/¾ cup *toovar dhal* or red
  split lentils
115g/4oz/½ cup basmati rice
1 large potato
1 large onion
30ml/2 tbsp oil
4 whole cloves
1.5ml/¼ tsp cumin seeds
1.5ml/¼ tsp ground turmeric
10ml/2 tsp salt
300ml/½ pint/1¼ cups water

1 Wash the *toovar dhal* or red split lentils and rice in several changes of cold water. Put into a bowl and cover with water. Leave to soak for 15 minutes then drain.

NUTRITIONAL NOTES	
Per Portion	
Energy	332Kcals/1396KJ
Fat	6.70g
Saturated Fat	0.76g
Carbohydrate	58.60g
Fibre	3.40g

2 Peel the potato, then cut it into 2.5cm/1in chunks.

3 Using a sharp knife, thinly slice the onion and set aside for later.

4 Heat the oil in a large heavy pan and fry the cloves and cumin seeds for 2 minutes until the seeds are beginning to splutter.

5 Add the onion and potato chunks and fry for 5 minutes. Add the lentils, rice, turmeric and salt and fry for a further 3 minutes.

6 Add the water. Bring to the boil, cover and simmer gently for 15–20 minutes until all the water has been absorbed and the potato chunks are tender. Leave to stand, covered, for about 10 minutes before serving.

COOK'S TIP

Red split lentils are widely available in most supermarkets. Before cooking they are salmon-coloured and they turn a pale, dull yellow during cooking. They have a mild, pleasant, nutty flavour.

Masala Chana

Chickpeas are used and cooked in a variety of ways all over the Indian sub-continent. Tamarind gives this dish a wonderfully sharp, tangy flavour.

INGREDIENTS

Serves 4

225g/8oz/1¼ cups dried chickpeas
50g/2oz tamarind stick
120ml/4fl oz/½ cup boiling water
30ml/2 tbsp oil
2.5ml/½ tsp cumin seeds
1 onion, finely chopped
2 garlic cloves, crushed
2.5cm/1in piece root ginger, grated
1 green chilli, finely chopped
5ml/1 tsp ground cumin
5ml/1 tsp ground coriander
1.5ml/¼ tsp ground turmeric
2.5ml/½ tsp salt
225g/8oz tomatoes, skinned and finely chopped
2.5ml/½ tsp garam masala
chopped chillies and chopped onion, to garnish

1 Put the chickpeas in a large bowl and cover with plenty of cold water. Leave to soak overnight.

___ COOK'S TIP ___

Tamarind is usually available in compressed blocks of pulp and seeds. To use, break off a small piece and soak it in a few spoonfuls of hot water for 15 minutes. Strain off the water, pressing some of the pulp through the sieve (strainer). Discard the rest of the pulp.

2 Drain the chickpeas and place in a large pan with double the volume of cold water. Bring to the boil and boil vigorously for 10 minutes. Skim off any scum. Lower the heat, cover and simmer for 1½–2 hours or until the chickpeas are soft.

3 Meanwhile, break up the tamarind and soak in the boiling water for about 15 minutes. Strain the tamarind into a bowl, discarding any stones and fibre.

NUTRITIONAL NOTES	
Per Portion	
Energy	313Kcals/1317KJ
Fat	9.40g
Saturated Fat	0.77g
Carbohydrate	44.60g
Fibre	1.50g

4 Heat the oil in a large heavy pan and fry the cumin seeds for 2 minutes until they splutter. Add the onion, garlic, ginger and chilli and fry for 5 minutes.

5 Add the cumin, coriander, turmeric and salt and fry for 3–4 minutes. Add the chopped tomatoes. Bring to the boil and simmer for 5 minutes.

6 Drain the chickpeas and add to the tomato mixture together with the garam masala and tamarind pulp. Cover and simmer gently for about 15 minutes. Garnish with the chopped chillies and onion before serving.

Spinach Dhal

Many different types of dhal are eaten in India and each region has its own speciality. This is a delicious, lightly spiced dish with a mild nutty flavour from the yellow lentils, which combine well with the spinach.

INGREDIENTS

Serves 4

175g/6oz/1 cup *chana dhal* or
  yellow split peas
175ml/6fl oz/¾ cup water
15ml/1 tbsp oil
1.5ml/¼ tsp black mustard seeds
1 onion, thinly sliced
2 garlic cloves, crushed
2.5cm/1in piece root ginger, grated
1 red chilli, finely chopped
275g/10oz frozen spinach, thawed
1.5ml/¼ tsp chilli powder
2.5ml/½ tsp ground coriander
2.5ml/½ tsp garam masala
2.5ml/½ tsp salt

1 Wash the *chana dhal* or split peas in several changes of cold water. Put into a bowl and cover with plenty of water. Leave to soak for 30 minutes.

2 Drain the split peas and put in a large pan with the water. Bring to the boil, cover and simmer for 20–25 minutes until soft.

NUTRITIONAL NOTES	
Per Portion	
Energy	183Kcals/778KJ
Fat	2.00g
Saturated Fat	0.44g
Carbohydrate	30.30g
Fibre	4.90g

3 Meanwhile, heat the oil in a large heavy frying pan and fry the mustard seeds for 2 minutes until they begin to splutter. Add the onion, garlic, ginger and chilli and fry for 5–6 minutes. Add the spinach and cook for 10 minutes or until the spinach is dry and the liquid has been absorbed. Stir in the remaining spices and salt and cook for 2–3 minutes.

4 Drain the split peas, add to the spinach and cook for about 5 minutes. Serve at once.

Balti Dhal with Green and Red Chillies

The white *urid dhal* which is used in this recipe should ideally be soaked overnight as this makes it easier to cook. Serve with freshly made chappatis.

INGREDIENTS

Serves 4

115g/4oz/½ cup *urid dhal*
10ml/2 tsp low fat spread
10ml/2 tsp oil
1 bay leaf
2 onions, sliced
1 piece cinnamon stick
2.5/1in piece root ginger, grated
2 garlic cloves
2 green chillies, seeded and sliced
   lengthways
2 red chillies, seeded and sliced
   lengthways
15ml/1 tbsp chopped fresh mint

1 Soak the dhal overnight in enough cold water to cover. Boil in water until the individual grains are soft enough to break into two. Set aside.

2 Heat the spread with the oil in a wok or heavy frying pan over medium heat. Fry the bay leaf with the onions and the cinnamon.

3 Add the ginger, whole garlic cloves and half the green and red chillies.

4 Drain almost all the water from the lentils. Add the lentils to the wok or frying pan, then the remaining green and red chillies and finally the fresh mint. Heat through briefly and serve.

NUTRITIONAL NOTES	
Per Portion	
Energy	159Kcals/663KJ
Fat	3.19g
Saturated Fat	0.51g
Carbohydrate	24.39g
Fibre	1.15g

COOK'S TIP

If you like your curries milder, replace some of the chillies with some finely chopped green or red (bell) peppers.

Balti Dhal with Spring Onions and Tomatoes

When cooked, *toor dhal* has a wonderfully rich texture, best appreciated if served with plain boiled rice. Fresh fenugreek leaves impart a stunning aroma.

Ingredients

Serves 4

115g/4oz/½ cup *toor dhal*
30ml/2 tbsp oil
1.5ml/¼ tsp onion seeds
1 medium bunch spring onions
   (scallions), roughly chopped
5ml/1 tsp crushed garlic
1.5ml/¼ tsp ground turmeric
7.5ml/1½ tsp crushed fresh root ginger
5ml/1 tsp chilli powder
30ml/2 tbsp fresh fenugreek leaves
5ml/1 tsp salt
150ml/¼ pint/⅔ cup water
6-8 cherry tomatoes
30ml/2 tbsp fresh coriander (cilantro)
   leaves
½ green (bell) pepper, seeded and sliced
15ml/1 tbsp lemon juice
shredded spring onion (scallions) tops
   and fresh coriander (cilantro) leaves,
   to garnish

--- Cook's Tip ---

Fresh fenugreek leaves are too bitter to use as a vegetable on their own but they are excellent mixed with pulses. If you cannot get fresh fenugreek leaves, use dried leaves which are available in most Indian shops.

Nutritional Notes	
Per Portion	
Energy	164Kcals/691KJ
Fat	6.40g
Saturated Fat	0.86g
Carbohydrate	19.10g
Fibre	1.10g

1 Cook the dhal in a pan of boiling water until soft and mushy. Drain and set aside.

2 Heat the oil with the onion seeds in a wok or heavy frying pan for a few seconds until hot.

3 Add the drained dhal to the wok or frying pan and stir-fry with the onion seeds for about 3 minutes.

4 Add the spring onions followed by the garlic, turmeric, ginger, chilli powder, fenugreek leaves and salt and continue to stir-fry for 5–7 minutes.

5 Pour in just enough of the water to loosen the mixture.

6 Add the whole cherry tomatoes, coriander leaves, green pepper and lemon juice. Stir well and serve garnished with shredded spring onion tops and some extra coriander leaves.

Mung Beans with Potatoes

Mung beans are one of the quicker-cooking pulses which do not require soaking and are very easy and convenient to use. In this recipe they are cooked with potatoes and Indian spices to give a tasty nutritious dish.

INGREDIENTS

Serves 4

175g/6oz/1 cup mung beans
750ml/1¼ pints/3 cups water
225g/8oz potatoes, cut into
   2cm/¾in chunks
30ml/2 tbsp oil
2.5ml/½ tsp cumin seeds
1 green chilli, finely chopped
1 garlic clove, crushed
2.5cm/1in piece root ginger,
   finely chopped
1.5ml/¼ tsp ground turmeric
2.5ml/½ tsp chilli powder
5ml/1 tsp salt
5ml/1 tsp sugar
4 curry leaves
5 tomatoes, skinned and
   finely chopped
15ml/1 tbsp tomato purée (paste)
curry leaves, to garnish
plain rice, to serve

1 Wash the beans. Bring to the boil in the water, cover and simmer until soft, about 30 minutes. Drain. Par-boil the potatoes for 10 minutes in another pan, then drain well.

2 Heat the oil in a heavy pan and fry the cumin seeds until they splutter. Add the chilli, garlic and ginger and fry for 3–4 minutes.

3 Add the turmeric, chilli powder, salt and sugar and cook for 2 minutes, stirring to prevent the mixture from sticking to the pan.

4 Add the 4 curry leaves, chopped tomatoes and tomato purée and simmer for about 5 minutes until the sauce thickens. Add the tomato sauce and the potatoes to the mung beans and mix well together. Garnish with the extra curry leaves and serve with plain boiled rice.

NUTRITIONAL NOTES	
Per Portion	
Energy	254Kcals/1070KJ
Fat	6.80g
Saturated Fat	0.89g
Carbohydrate	36.90g
Fibre	6.30g

Madras Sambal

There are many variations of this popular dish but it is regularly cooked in one form or another in almost every south-Indian home. You can use any combination of vegetables that are in season.

INGREDIENTS

Serves 4
225g/8oz/1 cup *toovar dhal* or red split lentils
600ml/1 pint/2½ cups water
2.5ml/½ tsp ground turmeric
2 large potatoes, cut into 2.5cm/1in chunks
30ml/2 tbsp oil
2.5ml/½ tsp black mustard seeds
1.5ml/¼ tsp fenugreek seeds
4 curry leaves
1 onion, thinly sliced
115g/4oz green beans, cut into 2.5cm/1in lengths
5ml/1 tsp salt
2.5ml/½ tsp chilli powder
15ml/1 tbsp lemon juice
toasted coconut, to garnish
Coriander Chutney, to serve

1 Wash the *toovar dhal* or lentils in several changes of water. Place in a heavy pan with the water and the turmeric. Bring to the boil, cover and simmer for 30–35 minutes until the lentils are soft.

NUTRITIONAL NOTES	
Per Portion	
Energy	335Kcals/1414KJ
Fat	6.10g
Saturated Fat	1.98g
Carbohydrate	55.70g
Fibre	5.60g

2 Par-boil the potatoes in a large pan of boiling water for 10 minutes. Drain well and set aside.

3 Heat the oil in a large frying pan and fry the mustard and fenugreek seeds and curry leaves for 2–3 minutes until the seeds begin to splutter. Add the sliced onion and the green beans and stir-fry for 7–8 minutes. Add the par-boiled potatoes and cook for a further 2 minutes.

4 Stir in the lentils with the salt, chilli powder and lemon juice and simmer for 2 minutes. Garnish with toasted coconut and serve with freshly made Coriander Chutney.

ACCOMPANIMENTS

Salads are an excellent choice as side dishes for anyone following a low fat diet, or you can increase the quantities for a main meal. And no Indian meal would be complete without a cooling raita or sweet relish. For the last course, you can still enjoy a guilt-free and refreshing finish to your meal, such as Melon and Strawberry Salad.

Fried Sesame Seed Chutney

This versatile chutney doubles as a dip, and also a sandwich filling.

INGREDIENTS

Serves 4

175g/6oz/³/₄ cup sesame seeds
5ml/1 tsp salt
120–150ml/4–5fl oz/½–²/₃ cup water
2 green chillies, seeded and diced
60ml/4 tbsp chopped fresh coriander
  (cilantro)
15ml/1 tbsp chopped fresh mint
15ml/1 tbsp tamarind paste
30ml/2 tbsp sugar
5ml/1 tsp oil
1.5ml/¼ tsp onion seeds
4 curry leaves

For the garnish

6 onion rings
1 green chilli, seeded and sliced
1 red chilli, seeded and sliced
15ml/1 tbsp fresh coriander (cilantro)
  leaves

1 Dry-roast the sesame seeds and leave to cool. Grind them in a coffee grinder to a grainy powder.

NUTRITIONAL NOTES	
Per Portion	
Energy	347Kcals/1438KJ
Fat	28.31g
Saturated Fat	4.03g
Carbohydrate	25.31g
Fibre	3.63g

2 Transfer the sesame powder to a bowl. Add the salt, water, diced chillies, coriander, mint, tamarind paste and sugar and, using a fork, mix everything together. Taste and adjust the seasoning if necessary; the mixture should have a sweet-and-sour flavour.

3 Heat the oil in a heavy pan and fry the onion seeds and curry leaves. Tip the sesame seed paste into the pan and stir-fry for about 45 seconds. Transfer the chutney to a serving dish amd allow to cool.

4 Garnish with onion rings, sliced green and red chillies and fresh coriander leaves and serve with your chosen curry.

Sweet-and-sour Raita

Raitas are traditionally served with most Indian meals as accompaniments which are cooling to the palate. They go particularly well with biryanis.

INGREDIENTS

Serves 4

475ml/16fl oz/2 cups natural (plain) low fat yogurt
5ml/1 tsp salt
5ml/1 tsp sugar
30ml/2 tbsp honey
7.5ml/1½ tsp mint sauce
30ml/2 tbsp roughly chopped fresh coriander (cilantro)
1 green chilli, seeded and finely chopped
1 medium onion, diced
50ml/2fl oz/¼ cup water

1 Pour the yogurt into a bowl and whisk it well. Add the salt, sugar, honey and mint sauce.

2 Taste to check the sweetness and add more honey, if desired.

3 Reserve a little chopped coriander for the garnish and add the rest to the yogurt mixture, with the chilli, onion and water.

NUTRITIONAL NOTES	
Per Portion	
Energy	128Kcals/541KJ
Fat	1.18g
Saturated Fat	0.64g
Carbohydrate	24.40g
Fibre	0.53g

4 Whisk once again and pour into a serving bowl. Garnish with the reserved coriander and place in the refrigerator until ready to serve.

_____ COOK'S TIP _____

A 5–10cm/2–4in piece of peeled, seeded and grated cucumber can also be added to raita. Alternatively, cut it into small dice.

Tomato and Onion Chutney

Chutneys are served with most
meat dishes in Indian cuisine.

INGREDIENTS

Serves 4

8 tomatoes
1 medium onion, chopped
45ml/3 tbsp brown sugar
5ml/1 tsp garam masala
5ml/1 tsp ginger powder
175ml/6fl oz/³⁄₄ cup malt vinegar
5ml/1 tsp salt
15ml/1 tbsp clear honey
natural (plain) low fat yogurt, sliced green
chilli and fresh mint leaves, to garnish

--- COOK'S TIP ---

This chutney will keep for about 2 weeks
in a covered jar in the refrigerator.

1 Wash the tomatoes and cut them
into quarters.

NUTRITIONAL NOTES	
Per Portion	
Energy	118Kcals/503KJ
Fat	0.66g
Saturated Fat	0.18g
Carbohydrate	43.90g
Fibre	2.34g

2 Place them with the onion in a
heavy pan.

3 Add the sugar, garam masala,
ginger, vinegar, salt and honey,
half-cover the pan with a lid and cook
over low heat for about 20 minutes.

4 Mash the tomatoes with a fork to
break them up, then continue to
cook on a slightly higher heat until the
chutney thickens. Serve chilled,
garnished with yogurt, sliced chilli
and mint leaves.

Sweet-and-sour Tomato and Onion Relish

This delicious relish can be served with any savoury meal.

INGREDIENTS

Serves 4

2 medium firm tomatoes
1 medium onion
1 green chilli
15ml/1 tbsp fresh mint leaves
15ml/1 tbsp fresh coriander (cilantro) leaves
2.5ml/½ tsp Tabasco sauce
15ml/1 tbsp clear honey
2.5ml/½ tsp salt
30ml/2 tbsp lime juice
15ml/1 tbsp natural (plain) low fat yogurt

1 Peel the tomatoes by placing them in hot water for a few seconds. Cut the tomatoes in half, discard the seeds and chop roughly. Set aside.

2 Roughly chop the onion, chilli, mint and fresh coriander.

3 Place the herb mixture in a food processor with the Tabasco sauce, honey, salt and lime juice. Add the tomatoes to this and grind everything together for a few seconds.

4 Pour into a small serving bowl. Finally, stir in the yogurt just before you serve the relish.

--- COOK'S TIP ---

This relish will keep for up to 1 week in the refrigerator: prepare up to the end of step 3 but do not add the yogurt until just before you want to serve it.

NUTRITIONAL NOTES	
Per Portion	
Energy	43Kcals/180KJ
Fat	0.29g
Saturated Fat	0.06g
Carbohydrate	9.43g
Fibre	0.96g

Sweet Potato and Carrot Salad

This salad has a sweet-and-sour taste, and can be served warm as part of a meal or eaten in a larger quantity as a main course.

INGREDIENTS

Serves 4

1 medium sweet potato
2 carrots, cut into thick diagonal slices
3 medium tomatoes
8–10 iceberg lettuce leaves
75g/3oz/½ cup canned chickpeas, drained

For the dressing
15ml/1 tbsp clear honey
90ml/6 tbsp natural (plain) low fat yogurt
2.5ml/½ tsp salt
5ml/1 tsp coarsely ground black pepper

For the garnish
15ml/1 tbsp walnuts
15ml/1 tbsp sultanas (golden raisins)
1 small onion, cut into rings

1 Peel the sweet potato and roughly dice. Boil until soft but not mushy, remove from the heat, cover the pan with a lid and set aside.

NUTRITIONAL NOTES	
Per Portion	
Energy	127Kcals/532KJ
Fat	3.70g
Saturated Fat	0.47g
Carbohydrate	20.60g
Fibre	3.10g

2 Boil the carrots for just a few minutes, making sure that they remain crunchy. Add the carrots to the sweet potatoes.

3 Drain the water from the sweet potatoes and carrots and place together in a bowl.

4 Slice the tops off the tomatoes, then scoop out and discard the seeds. Roughly chop the flesh.

_____ COOK'S TIP _____

The skin of sweet potatoes may be pink or orangey yellow and the flesh can range from mealy to moist and from almost white to deep yellow in colour. It is best to boil or bake sweet potatoes in their skins if possible, as some varieties turn a dullish colour if boiled unpeeled.

5 Line a glass bowl with the lettuce leaves. Mix together the sweet potatoes, carrots, chickpeas and tomatoes and place in the bowl.

6 Blend together all the dressing ingredients and beat using a fork.

7 Garnish the salad with the walnuts, sultanas and onion rings. Pour the dressing over the salad or serve it in a separate bowl, if wished.

Spinach and Mushroom Salad

This salad is especially good served with Glazed Garlic Prawns (shrimp) or any other seafood curry. It is also delicious served on its own with some warm naan bread as a light lunch-time snack.

INGREDIENTS

Serves 4
10 baby corn cobs
115g/4oz mushrooms
2 medium tomatoes
20 small spinach leaves
8-10 onion rings
25g/1oz salad cress (optional)
salt and black pepper
fresh coriander (cilantro) sprigs and lime slices, to garnish (optional)

1 Halve the baby corn cobs and slice the mushrooms and tomatoes.

2 Arrange all the salad ingredients in a bowl. Season with salt and pepper and garnish with fresh coriander and lime slices, if wished.

NUTRITIONAL NOTES	
Per Portion	
Energy	25Kcals/103KJ
Fat	0.60g
Saturated Fat	0.09g
Carbohydrate	2.80g
Fibre	1.80g

_____ COOK'S TIP _____

Baby corn can be eaten whole or sliced in half lengthways. Don't overcook them or they will lose their sweetness and be tough. To use in salads, cook for about 3 minutes.

Nutty Salad

INGREDIENTS

Serves 4
1 medium onion, cut into 12 rings
115g/4oz/½ cup canned red kidney beans, drained
1 green courgette (zucchini), sliced
1 yellow courgette (zucchini), sliced
50g/2oz/⅔ cup pasta shells, cooked
50g/2oz/½ cup cashew nuts
25g/1oz/¼ cup peanuts
fresh coriander (cilantro) and lime wedges, to garnish

For the dressing
115g/4oz low fat fromage frais or crème fraîche
30ml/2 tbsp natural (plain) low fat yogurt
1 fresh green chilli, chopped
15ml/1 tbsp chopped coriander (cilantro)
2.5ml/½ tsp salt
2.5ml/½ tsp crushed black peppercorns
2.5ml/½ tsp crushed dried red chillies
15ml/1 tbsp lemon juice

1 Arrange the onion rings, kidney beans, courgette slices and pasta in a salad dish and sprinkle the cashew nuts and peanuts over the top.

2 In a separate bowl, blend together the fromage frais or crème fraîche, yogurt, green chilli, fresh coriander and salt and beat well using a fork.

3 Sprinkle the crushed peppercorns, red chillies and lemon juice over the dressing. Garnish the salad with fresh coriander and lime wedges and serve with the dressing.

NUTRITIONAL NOTES	
Per Portion	
Energy	199Kcals/829KJ
Fat	11.60g
Saturated Fat	2.63g
Carbohydrate	15.20g
Fibre	2.90g

_____ COOK'S TIP _____

Fromage frais or crème fraîche mixed with yogurt makes a deliciously smooth and creamy, low fat dressing which perfectly complements the nuttiness of this salad.

Yogurt Salad

A delicious salad with a yogurt base, this is really an Eastern version of coleslaw.

INGREDIENTS

Serves 4

350ml/12fl oz/1½ cups natural (plain) low fat yogurt
10ml/2 tsp clear honey
2 medium carrots, thickly sliced
2 spring onions (scallions), roughly chopped
115g/4oz/1½ cups cabbage, finely shredded
50g/2oz/⅓ cup sultanas (golden raisins)
50g/2oz/½ cup cashew nuts (optional)
16 white grapes, halved
2.5ml/½ tsp salt
5ml/1 tsp chopped fresh mint

1 Using a fork, beat the yogurt in a bowl with the honey.

2 Mix together the carrots, spring onions, cabbage, sultanas, cashew nuts (if you are using them), grapes, salt and chopped mint.

3 Pour the sweetened yogurt mixture over the salad, blend everything together with a fork and serve.

NUTRITIONAL NOTES	
Per Portion	
Energy	119Kcals/503KJ
Fat	0.90g
Saturated Fat	0.49g
Carbohydrate	23.40g
Fibre	1.80g

Spicy Baby Vegetable Salad

This warm vegetable salad makes an excellent accompaniment to almost any main course dish.

INGREDIENTS

Serves 6

10 baby potatoes, halved
15 baby carrots
10 baby courgettes (zucchini)
115g/4oz/1½ cups button (white) mushrooms

For the dressing

45ml/3 tbsp lemon juice
25ml/1½ tbsp oil
15ml/1 tbsp chopped fresh coriander (cilantro)
5ml/1 tsp salt
2 small green chillies, finely sliced

1 Boil the potatoes, carrots and courgettes in water until tender. Drain them and place in a serving dish with the mushrooms.

2 In a separate bowl, mix together all the ingredients for the dressing.

3 Toss the vegetables in the dressing and serve immediately.

NUTRITIONAL NOTES	
Per Portion	
Energy	73Kcals/308KJ
Fat	3.10g
Saturated Fat	0.39g
Carbohydrate	10.10g
Fibre	1.50g

_____ COOK'S TIP _____

As well as looking extremely attractive, the tiny baby vegetables give this salad a lovely flavour. Other baby vegetables, such as leeks, miniature corn cobs or egg-sized cauliflowers can be used just as well.

Ground Rice Pudding

This delicious and light ground rice pudding is the perfect end to a spicy meal. It can be served either hot or cold.

INGREDIENTS

Serves 4–6

50g/2oz/½ cup coarsely ground rice
4 green cardamom pods, crushed
900ml/1½ pints/3¾ cups semi-
    skimmed (low-fat) milk
90ml/6 tbsp sugar
15ml/1 tbsp rose water
15ml/1 tbsp crushed pistachio nuts,
    to garnish

1 pan with the cardamoms. Add 600ml/1 pint/2½ cups milk and bring to the boil over medium heat, stirring occasionally.

2 Add the remaining milk and cook over medium heat for about 10 minutes or until the rice mixture thickens to the consistency of a creamy chicken soup.

3 Stir in the sugar and rose water and continue to cook for a further 2 minutes. Serve garnished with the pistachio nuts.

—————— COOK'S TIP ——————

Rose water is a distillation of scented rose petals which has the intense fragrance and flavour of roses. It is a popular flavouring in Indian cooking. Use it cautiously, adding just enough to suit your taste.

NUTRITIONAL NOTES
Per Portion

Energy	260Kcals/1102KJ
Fat	5.80g
Saturated Fat	2.53g
Carbohydrate	46.00g
Fibre	0.30g

Vermicelli

Indian vermicelli, made from wheat, is much finer than Italian vermicelli and is readily available from Asian stores.

INGREDIENTS

Serves 4

115g/4oz/1 cup vermicelli
1.2 litres/2 pints/5 cups water
2.5ml/½ tsp saffron strands
15ml/1 tbsp sugar
60ml/4 tbsp low fat fromage frais or crème fraîche, to serve (optional)

For the garnish

15ml/1 tbsp shredded fresh or desiccated (dry unsweetened shredded) coconut
15ml/1 tbsp flaked (sliced) almonds
15ml/1 tbsp chopped pistachio nuts
15ml/1 tbsp sugar

1 Crush the vermicelli in your hands and place in a pan. Pour in the water, add the saffron and bring to the boil. Boil for about 5 minutes.

2 Stir in the sugar and continue cooking until the water has evaporated. Strain if necessary, to remove any excess liquid.

3 Place the vermicelli in a serving dish and garnish with the coconut, almonds, pistachio nuts and sugar. Serve with fromage frais, if wished.

_____ COOK'S TIP _____

You can use a variety of fruits instead of nuts to garnish this dessert. Try a few soft fruits such as blackberries, raspberries or strawberries, or add some chopped dried apricots or sultanas (golden raisins).

NUTRITIONAL NOTES	
Per Portion	
Energy	196Kcals/822KJ
Fat	6.60g
Saturated Fat	2.27g
Carbohydrate	31.80g
Fibre	0.80g

Melon and Strawberry Salad

A beautiful and colourful fruit salad, this is suitable to serve as a refreshing appetizer or to round off a spicy meal.

INGREDIENTS

Serves 4
1 galia melon
1 honeydew melon
½ watermelon
225g/8oz/2 cups fresh strawberries
15ml/1 tbsp lemon juice
15ml/1 tbsp clear honey
15ml/1 tbsp chopped fresh mint

1 Prepare the melons by cutting them in half and discarding the seeds. Use a melon ball to scoop out the flesh into balls or a knife to cut it into cubes. Place these in a fruit bowl.

2 Rinse and take the stems off the strawberries, cut the fruit in half and add them to the bowl.

3 Mix together the lemon juice and honey and add 15ml/1 tbsp water to make this easier to pour over the fruit. Mix into the fruit gently.

4 Sprinkle the chopped mint over the top of the fruit and serve.

NUTRITIONAL NOTES
Per Portion

Energy	114Kcals/482KJ
Fat	0.70g
Saturated Fat	0.00g
Carbohydrate	26.50g
Fibre	1.60g

—————— COOK'S TIP ——————

Use whichever melons are available: replace galia with cantaloupe or watermelon with charentais, for example. Try to choose three melons with a variation in colour for an attractive effect.

Caramel Custard with Fresh Fruit

A creamy caramel dessert is a wonderful way to end a meal. It is light and delicious, and this recipe is very simple.

INGREDIENTS

Serves 6
For the caramel
30ml/2 tbsp sugar
30ml/2 tbsp water

For the custard
6 eggs
4 drops vanilla extract
120–150ml/8–10 tbsp sugar
750ml/1¼ pints/3 cups semi-
   skimmed (low-fat) milk
fresh fruit, such as strawberries,
   blueberries, orange and banana
   slices and raspberries, to serve

1 To make the caramel, place the sugar and water in a heavy pan and heat until the sugar has dissolved and the mixture is bubbling and pale gold in colour. Pour carefully into a 1.2 litre/2 pint/5 cup soufflé dish. Leave to cool.

2 Preheat the oven to 180°C/350°F/ Gas 4. To make the custard, break the eggs into a medium mixing bowl and whisk until frothy.

COOK'S TIP

Use vanilla extract rather than synthetic vanilla flavouring for this custard as the flavour is much better; remember extract is very strong and you only need a few drops.

3 Stir in the vanilla extract and gradually add the sugar, then the milk, whisking continuously.

4 Pour the custard over the top of the caramel.

5 Cook the custard in the oven for 35–40 minutes. Remove from the oven and leave to cool for 30 minutes or until the mixture is set.

6 Loosen the custard from the sides of the dish with a knife. Place a serving dish upside-down on top of the soufflé dish and invert, giving a gentle shake if necessary to turn out the custard on to the serving dish.

7 Arrange any fresh fruit of your choice around the custard on the serving dish and serve immediately.

NUTRITIONAL NOTES	
Per Portion	
Energy	194Kcals/823KJ
Fat	4.70g
Saturated Fat	2.01g
Carbohydrate	32.90g
Fibre	0.00g

Lassi

Lassi is a very popular drink in both India and Pakistan. It is available not only from roadside cafés but is also a great favourite in good restaurants and hotels. There is no substitute for this drink, especially on a hot day. It is particularly ideal served with hot dishes as it helps the body to digest spicy food.

INGREDIENTS

Serves 4

300ml/½ pint/1¼ cups natural (plain) low fat yogurt
5ml/1 tsp sugar, or to taste
300ml/½ pint/1¼ cups water
30ml/2 tbsp puréed fruit (optional)
15ml/1 tbsp crushed pistachio nuts, to garnish

1 Place the yogurt in a jug and whisk until frothy. Add the sugar.

NUTRITIONAL NOTES	
Per Portion	
Energy	70Kcals/296KJ
Fat	2.60g
Saturated Fat	0.63g
Carbohydrate	7.50g
Fibre	0.00g

2 Pour in the water and the puréed fruit, if using, and continue to whisk for 2 minutes. Pour the lassi into serving glasses and serve chilled, decorated with crushed pistachio nuts.

_____ COOK'S TIP _____

To make a savoury lassi, omit the sugar and fruit and season to taste with lemon juice, ground cumin and salt. Garnish with mint.

Almond Sherbet

Traditionally, this drink was always made in the month of Ramadan to break the fast. It should be served chilled.

INGREDIENTS

Serves 4

50g/2oz/½ cup ground almonds
600ml/1 pint/2½ cups semi-skimmed (low-fat) milk
10ml/2 tsp sugar, or to taste

NUTRITIONAL NOTES	
Per Portion	
Energy	155Kcals/651KJ
Fat	9.40g
Saturated Fat	2.04g
Carbohydrate	11.00g
Fibre	0.90g

1 Put the ground almonds into a serving jug.

_____ COOK'S TIP _____

Refreshing, cooling drinks are the perfect accompaniment to spicy Indian dishes. Similar drinks are made with fruit juices flavoured with chopped fresh mint.

2 Pour in the semi-skimmed milk and add the sugar; stir to mix. Taste for sweetness and serve chilled.

Index

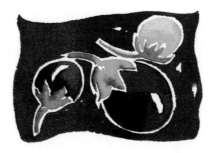